The Nuts and Bolts of Writing

Michael Legat was born in London and educated at Whitgift School, South Croydon. He was for many years Editorial Director of a paperback publishing house, and later occupied the same position in a hardcover publishing firm. In 1978 he turned to writing, since when he has published five novels, including *Mario's Vineyard* and *The Silk Maker*, a book on amateur drama, the highly acclaimed *An Author's Guide to Publishing* and the equally successful *Writing For Pleasure and Profit*, and *The Illustrated Dictionary of Western Literature*.

He teaches creative writing and lectures widely. He has served on the Management Committee of the Society of Authors and on the Literature Advisory Panel of South-East Arts, and is currently a Director of the Authors' Licensing and Collection Society and of the Copyright Licensing Agency.

Michael Legat lives with his wife and a comical dog in Horsted Keynes, Sussex.

Also by Michael Legat

non-fiction
Dear Author...
An Author's Guide to Publishing
Writing for Pleasure and Profit
The Illustrated Dictionary of Western Literature
Putting on a Play

novels
Mario's Vineyard
The Silver Fountain
The Shapiro Diamond
The Silk Maker
The Cast Iron Man

The Nuts and Bolts
of Writing

808·
042
LEG

© Michael Legat 1989
First published in Great Britain 1989
Reprinted 1990

Robert Hale Limited
Clerkenwell House
Clerkenwell Green
London EC1R 0HT

British Library Cataloguing in Publication Data

Legat, Michael
  The nuts and bolts of writing.
  1. English language. Writing skills
  I. Title
  808'.042'076

  ISBN 0-7090-3450-4 (Paperback)
       0-7090-3748-1 (Cased)

Photoset in Sabon by Derek Doyle & Associates
Printed in Great Britain by
St Edmundsbury Press Limited, Bury St Edmunds, Suffolk
Bound by WBC Bookbinders

Contents

This book is dedicated in friendship and gratitude
to John Hale
in the hope that it will achieve its aim
and also
to John McLaughlin
whose advice I so much appreciate

Introduction

This book originated in a cry of mixed irritation and despair from my publisher. 'You would not believe', he said, 'the poor standard of the typescripts submitted for our consideration. I don't mean the actual content of the books, but the spelling, the punctuation, the grammar, and the presentation. There are plenty of books which tell would-be writers how to write novels or non-fiction or articles, including your own *Writing for Pleasure and Profit*, but there's a real need for something on what I would call the nuts and bolts of writing.'

No sensible author ignores such a suggestion from a publisher, especially when he's right. Many excellent books on spelling, punctuation and grammar already exist, but most of them seem to have a strong flavour of the text book, rather than being aimed at someone who is trying to get work published, and certainly none of these specialist works also covers the way to submit a typescript or information on such subjects as literary agents and organizations for authors.

The Nuts and Bolts of Writing attempts to fill the gap.

M.L.

PART ONE

The Tools Of The Trade

Let us therefore agree ... that a reasonably good standard of writing is a mark not of preciosity but of good sense, not of prissiness but of efficiency; that such a standard can be attained by anyone with a little effort; that the effort will be worthwhile ...; that it requires neither hairsplitting nor self-consciousness but merely a willingness to acquire good habits.

Sir Ernest Gowers

1   Punctuation

When we speak we use pauses and inflexions to make our meaning clear. The pauses may be very slight – almost imperceptible – and the inflexions may be quite subtle variations in tone, but they can make a great difference to the sense of our words. For instance, if we say, 'He is tall and handsome,' we are making a straightforward statement in which neither his height nor his good looks takes precedence over the other. But if we say, 'He is tall *and* handsome,' the emphasis puts extra weight on the second adjective, and suggests as the thought behind the words, 'He is not only tall, but handsome, too.' Yet again, if we say, 'He is tall – (*slight pause*) and handsome,' we are expressing masculine beauty as a kind of extra piece of information, almost as an afterthought. Inflexions also make it clear whether we are making a statement or asking a question. If we say, 'The dog is trained' with a downward inflexion on the last word, it is a statement, but if there is an upward inflexion, it becomes a question. And by stressing certain words, we obtain yet other variations: 'The *dog* is trained' suggests that some other animal or person (perhaps the dog's owner) isn't trained; while 'The dog *is* trained' is a particularly emphatic statement.

In writing, these pauses and inflexions are replaced by punctuation, which makes sense of what we write, avoids confusion and indicates expression.

Take, for instance, the following unpunctuated passage:

He told me where he was going to see James and I replied that he might see Brenda there at the same time the dog started barking again I had to shout as I asked will you tell him I I tried to quieten the dog but I failed to shut him up of course I should have given him a bone I know Bill did not hear me I thought he smiled as he went away without my having had a chance to question him for the second time I went home dissatisfied.

11

As written it is impossible to tell how that is to be read, and although one can just about make sense of it, the addition of punctuation can not only clarify it, but can be used to give it different meanings.

For instance, it could be punctuated as follows:

> He told me where he was going – to see James – and I replied that he might see Brenda there. At the same time the dog started barking. Again I had to shout as I asked, 'Will you tell him I –?' I tried to quieten the dog, but I failed; to shut him up, of course, I should have given him a bone. I know Bill did not hear me. I thought he smiled as he went away, without my having had a chance to question him. For the second time, I went home dissatisfied.

Alternatively, it could be punctuated like this:

> He told me where he was going to see James, and I replied that he might see Brenda there at the same time. The dog started barking again. I had to shout as I asked, 'Will you tell him I ... I tried to quieten the dog, but I failed to shut him up? Of course, I should have given him a bone, I know.' Bill did not hear me, I thought. He smiled as he went away. Without my having had a chance to question him for the second time, I went home dissatisfied.

Several other variations are possible, especially if we add the underlining of certain words (which should really be considered as a form of punctuation) to give particular emphasis to them, and each new version will have its own shades of meaning.

In the course of this chapter so far half a dozen or so punctuation marks have been used. There are many more. In the following pages, each of them and its various functions will be examined.

The Full Stop

Full stops are used at the end of statements which are neither interrogatory nor exclamatory. They separate sentences, especially when the sentences present different ideas or thoughts: *The cat sat on the mat. The dog watched it. The cat purred. The dog growled.* Reading those four sentences aloud, you will probably insert a more-than-slight pause between each one; in writing, such pauses almost always demand a full stop (or at least a semi-colon – see below). They can be used in a somewhat unusual way to create a special effect, as in: *He was free. Rich. Happy. And very drunk.* This produces a quite different, more emphatic impression from the more conventional style of: *He was free, rich, happy, and very drunk.*

Full stops are also used in abbreviations: *U.N.O., B.B.C., etc., Mrs., Dr.* Increasingly, however, full stops are omitted in abbreviations, and *UNO, BBC, Mrs, Dr* are acceptable forms.

The Comma

The comma is used on numerous occasions:

1. To separate the items in a list, as in the sentence quoted above: *He was free, rich, happy, and very drunk.* Or: *The drinks available before lunch included white wine, gin and tonic, scotch and soda, orange juice, and spring water.* The question of whether there should be a comma before the last 'and' in such lists is a difficult one. If the final item needs to be stressed, or contrasts with the previous word (as in 'and very drunk'), or if the final item is a group of words which represents a single object but in which 'and' appears, (as in 'gin and tonic' or 'scotch and soda', if they had come at the end of the sentence), or if there is likely to be ambiguity (if you omit the comma after 'orange juice' do you mean that 'orange juice' and 'spring water' are alternatives, or form one drink?), it is better to include the comma before the final 'and'; indeed you will never be wrong to do so. It is, however, possible and usual to omit it in such a list as: *The jewellery consisted of diamonds, rubies, emeralds, sapphires and pearls.* The list can also consist of a series of phrases: *He was aware of the brilliant sunlight, the dark shadows of the trees, the lack of a wind, and the stillness of the village.* Or a series of clauses: *She was the kind of woman who never complained, who thought only of his welfare, who would follow him anywhere, and who was happy however badly he treated her.* Or: *She hurried down the street, ran into the baker's, and bought a loaf, two macaroons and a cherry cake. Then she went to the take-away, waited in the queue, and eventually emerged with packets of fried chicken, individual steak-and-kidney pies, and fish and chips.*

2. To separate two or more descriptions appearing in sequence of the same thing: *the ripe, golden sheaves of corn.* Or: *the happiest, funniest, most exciting show in town.* Or: *My wife,*

Rosetta, will accompany me. But note that the comma is not always necessary. We write, for example: *the little black dog.* Or: *the well-known English author.* You can usually tell when the comma is necessary and when it can be omitted if you say the words aloud. You would not pause after 'little' when saying 'the little black dog', so no comma is needed; on the other hand, you would almost certainly make a very slight break between 'ripe' and 'golden' so a comma is required in that case.

3. Before or after the name of someone to whom a line of dialogue is addressed (and both before and after the name if it comes in the middle of the sentence): *'What's the matter, Kevin? Darling, please be reasonable.'* *'All I wanted, Carol, was for you to be happy.'*

4. Before or after (and, if necessary, both before and after) direct speech which is attributed to a person: *He said, 'I don't understand.'* *'You wouldn't,' she replied.* Or: *'All I wanted,' he began, 'was for you to be happy,' and he laughed bitterly.* Note that the comma which comes before the attribution (that is, 'he said' or 'he began' or 'she replied'), or before the continuation of the sentence (as in 'and he laughed bitterly'), appears inside the quotation marks.

5. To separate a phrase or clause which is subsidiary to the main sentence: *In her haste, she had forgotten to get anything to drink.* Or: *It was a forlorn hope, which she was foolish to cherish.* Note that while the comma is virtually mandatory if the subsidiary clause or phrase comes at the beginning of a sentence, it may sometimes be omitted when the clause or phrase appears in the middle of the sentence: *Somewhat despairingly, she hoped that he would not notice,* but *She hoped somewhat despairingly that he would not notice.* If you do separate such a phrase by placing a comma in front of it, then you must also insert one at the end of the phrase: *She hoped, somewhat despairingly, that he would not notice.* The same applies if it is a clause appearing in the middle of the sentence: *The take-away food, which was still hot, would be on the table in a moment.* Equally, it would be wrong to insert the comma at the end of the phrase or clause in such cases without putting one in before it. The commas are acting rather like brackets, and must be opened and closed, as it were. As a special point, it is worth noting that 'however' almost always needs the comma wherever it occurs in the sentence: *However, he saw it at once,* or *He saw it, however, at once.*

6. To separate sentences joined by the conjunctions 'and' or 'but', particularly when the sentences have different subjects. *They*

attacked again, but our defence was strong. Or: *She looked at him defiantly, but he did not notice.* On the other hand, when a sentence has a single subject controlling two verbs, the comma after 'and' may be omitted: *Emma put down her book and sipped thoughtfully at her cup of tea.* Or: *He grabbed the bag and ran off down the street.*

Commas are not 'strong' enough to separate sentences which are not joined by conjunctions. So it is incorrect to write, for example: *She shut the door, he turned towards her.* The two sentences in that example need to be separated by a full stop or a semi-colon. On the other hand, commas can be used if what you are writing is, in effect, a list, especially if you are aiming at a special effect. For instance: *She shut the door, the cat ran towards him, he grabbed at it and missed, and Grandma, sitting in the corner, gave a little scream.* By running those sentences together and using commas instead of full stops, you have added a sense of everything happening at once, which would not have been so apparent if you had used full stops.

Note also the difference between *He picked up the card which was by his hand*, and *He picked up the card, which was by his hand*. The first sentence, without the comma, suggests that he picked up the nearest of several cards; the insertion of the comma in the second sentence implies that there was only one card, which was by his hand.

Correct use of the comma is very difficult, and the tendency among most writers is to use too many. If your work is spotted all over with commas, there are three tests you might try: firstly, are the commas there to separate items in a list, before or after the attributions in dialogue, before or after the name of persons addressed in dialogue? If so, they will probably have to stay, for such commas are virtually mandatory. Secondly, looking at the remaining commas, will the meaning remain clear and as you intend if you take out the commas? If so, you can probably remove some or all of them. Thirdly, try reading the work aloud; where you pause (unless you have stopped simply because you have run out of breath), you will probably need a punctuation mark – a full stop (or possibly a semi-colon, a colon, or the appropriate signs if it is a question or an exclamation), but a comma if the pause is a slight one.

The Semi-Colon

The semi-colon is used to separate two or more sentences which are usually related by subject matter. It often, therefore, takes the place of 'and' or 'but'. For example: *The pause indicated by a semi-colon is considerably longer than that suggested by a comma; on the other hand, it is less weighty than a full stop; by linking sentences, it can sometimes give a smoother effect than a series of full stops.* Or: *He had forgotten to turn out the light; the door should have been closed, too.* The four short sentences quoted in the section on the full stop above could also have been written as: *The cat sat on the mat; the dog watched it; the cat purred; the dog growled.*

Many writers forget or hesitate to use the semi-colon, perhaps because they feel that it is unusual nowadays and therefore draws unwanted attention to itself. It is true that a conscious effort is needed to insert a semi-colon; before many years have passed it may even be considered archaic. This is a pity, because it is an extremely useful punctuation mark. It is rarely seen in dialogue, where the full stop seems more natural, but in prose it has a genuine function to perform and can add variety and a change of rhythm to your work.

The Colon

The colon is used:

1. To introduce a list or an example. For instance: *The ingredients for Pineapple Surprise are: ½ fresh pineapple, 1–2 tablespoons water, 50g icing sugar. Method: Scoop out the pineapple ...*

2. To introduce dialogue. For example: *He shouted: 'What's the matter?'* (But note that the comma is more usual in such cases.) The colon is particularly useful if introducing a quotation which would not normally follow such a word as 'said' or 'wrote'. For example: *There is a proverb which seems apt at this time: 'Many a true word is spoken in jest.'*

3. To introduce an explanation or amplification of a statement. For example: *She gave her recipe for a prosperous Britain: freedom from unnecessary controls.* Or: *He realised at once where she had gone: to her mother's.*

It is quite common to use a dash after a colon, the two marks being joined together, but the only virtue in this usage is at the end of a paragraph to draw particular attention to the fact that a list follows. Even then, it is not really necessary.

The Question Mark

The question mark comes at the end of a direct question. For example: *Why?* Or: *How do you do?* (It must be admitted, however, that if we are old-fashioned enough to say 'How do you do?' when introduced, we do not expect a direct reply, other than perhaps a 'How do you do?' in return, and the question has turned into a formal way of saying 'Hello'. It could be argued, therefore, that a full stop would be more appropriate, but it is in fact a question and should be shown as such.)

The question mark also transforms into a question a group of words which would otherwise appear to be a statement. For example: the question mark in *He said he was coming?* tells us to read it as a question.

Two problems arise with question marks. The first is the matter of indirect speech. Question marks should not be used. For example: *He asked if we had seen it.* Or: *Uppermost in his mind was the question of whether they should go.* But if you say, *Uppermost in his mind was the question: should they go?* the question mark goes in.

The second difficulty arises with a long and complex sentence which begins with a question, but ends with a statement. For example, if you were to write, *May I ask whether this is really so, since it is contrary to all previous advice that I have received, and until you convince me that you are right, I shall continue to withhold payment,* you should put a question mark at the end however out of place it may seem. (It might be preferable to rephrase the sentence to read: *May I ask whether this is really so? It is contrary to all previous advice …*)

The Exclamation Mark

The exclamation mark is used after exclamations like *Oh!*, or *Oh dear!*, or *Hell's bells!*, and to add emphasis to commands or statements such as *Go away!* or *I didn't!*.

It is also used to express the idea that something is extraordinary or surprising. For example, at the end of a story about someone who believed that she had heard burglars in the house: *It was only a mouse!* Or: *Shakespeare's vocabulary contained no fewer than thirty thousand words!*

While the use of exclamation marks is legitimate, and often essential, in dialogue, in order to convey the sound, the expression, the emotion which the author intends the reader to understand, their appearance in other circumstances is largely to be avoided. No one minds if, in a letter to a friend, you use exclamation marks, even in threes (*My dear, I was flabbergasted!!!*), and there may be some place for them in an article written in a popular style. In a book or in any piece of more serious writing, however, an exclamation mark appearing other than in dialogue can often seem to be an intrusion. It is as though the author were saying, 'Isn't that strange?', 'Wasn't that funny?' Readers are quite capable of making such judgments for themselves, and usually prefer to do so.

The Dash

The dash is an interesting punctuation mark. In some instances its use is entirely legitimate, but in others, many purists consider it to be a lazy way of punctuating which should be confined, like triple exclamation marks, to informal correspondence. It is, in fact, not to be sneered at, for even at its sloppiest, it can add certain qualities to your writing which no other punctuation mark can exactly provide.

It is used in dialogue, entirely in its own right, as it were, to indicate a speech which has been interrupted. For example: '*I heard it yesterday,*' *he said.* '*I was in the office, and Jeremy –*' *He broke off as the door opened.* Or: '*Let me explain. I was –*' '*I don't want to hear your explanations!*' The dash is sometimes used to indicate a speech which is not completed, rather than one which is actually interrupted, but I prefer to use three full stops (see below) in such cases, as I also do to indicate hesitancy in a speaker.

Another use of the dash (or sometimes a series of dashes) is to indicate a word which has been censored, and it is quite usual to substitute a dash for each letter of the offending word. For example: '*– – – – you!*' *he said*. The Victorians often used dashes in words like *d*—— (for 'damn') or *d*——*d* (for 'damned'). Nowadays, since the so-called 'four-letter words' are freely used, the device is rarely seen. Similarly, while writers fifty or more years ago would often refer to a character in a story as, for instance, *Dr F*——, or *a lady whom I shall call M*——, we tend now to be less coy, and even if, for some reason, we wish not to give a character his or her full name, we would probably write 'M.', rather than 'M——'.

It is when the dash replaces other punctuation marks that some people disapprove. It can be used, for instance:

1. In place of commas. *He took the suitcase, the bunch of*

flowers – and my umbrella – when he left. An additional emphasis has been placed on the umbrella by the use of the dashes. Note that there is a dash both before and after the interpolation. It would be wrong, or at least would give a different sense to the sentence to write, *He took the suitcase, the bunch of flowers – and my umbrella when he left.*

2. In place of brackets. *The use of dashes – whether you like them or not – is widely accepted.* The difference here is a subtle one. If 'whether you like them or not' had been placed in brackets, the effect would have been something like an 'aside' in the theatre; it would have isolated the words from the rest of the sentence rather more strongly than the dashes do. Again, don't forget to put in the closing dash after the interpolation, or parenthesis.

3. In place of a semi-colon or full stop. *Her head was swimming – the whole room was going round.* This adds an immediacy to the linked sentences which would not be achieved by either a semi-colon or a full stop.

4. In place of a colon. For example: *The decoration of the Christmas tree, the stuffing of the turkey, the sudden recollection that he had forgotten the wine, and the run to the off-licence to buy it – all these tasks filled his Christmas eve.* Or: *Everything he needed was there – wig, make-up, dark glasses and even a white walking-stick.* These seem to me entirely acceptable usages.

When typing your work, you can indicate a dash in several ways. If you use a single dash you must put a space before it and after it (for example: *flowers – and*), for otherwise it could be confused with a hyphen. If you use a double dash, you can do so either with spaces either side or without (for example: *flowers — and* or *flowers—and*). There is no need to put a comma in front of a dash.

Brackets

Brackets are sometimes called 'parentheses'. A 'parenthesis' is an interpolation – something which is often enclosed in brackets (although it can also be within dashes or commas) – and the plural of the term has come to be applied to the brackets themselves.

Brackets are used to surround an interpolation in a sentence which demands to be marked as such. There have been many instances of their use already in this chapter. The essential character of material placed in brackets is that, although it is relevant to what is being said, and, indeed, may be very important, it can be removed from the sentence without altering the sense. As already suggested in the section on the dash above, the use of brackets tends to separate their contents rather more strongly from the surrounding material than dashes would do.

Brackets are frequently used for 'asides', often with comic effect: *He said that he was young (which was true) and innocent (which was not).*

Three Full Stops

Three full stops in a row form a useful device to indicate an unfinished sentence, particularly in dialogue. For example: *'I have been wondering about ....'* Lost in thought, he did not finish the sentence*. The three dots always suggest to me a trailing off, rather than an abruptly interrupted speech.

Three full stops can also be effective in conveying hesitancy in dialogue. For example: *'I ... I don't know.'* Or: *'The ... er ... the fact ... is ... well ... I hesitate to ... er ... say exactly.'*

These usages are not properly examples of an ellipsis, which is the term given to three full stops when they indicate the omission of a word or words, often in reporting a speech. For example: *The Chancellor stated that 'in view of the state of the economy ... the pound will have to be devalued.'* The missing words might be *which has performed less well than expected.* An ellipsis can also sometimes be used at the end of a sentence. For example: *It was an unworthy thought, but ....* The reader will understand the rest of the sentence, which might be *he could not prevent himself from thinking it.* Or it is used at the end of a list. For example: *The circus arrived with the swings, the hoop-la stalls, the caravans, the blaring music, the fairground people ...* The unwritten words in this case are *and all the rest of the elements which make up a travelling circus.*

The observant reader will have noticed that in some of the examples above the three full stops have turned into four. It is conventional, when the ellipsis falls at the end of a sentence, to add the full stop which would have been there anyway, if you see what I mean. When you are typing your work, there is no need ever to put more than three full stops in a row, or four if they come at the end of a sentence. They will do the work just as efficiently as a dozen.

Be careful not to use three full stops too often. Their frequent repetition can be irritating.

The Apostrophe

The best-known use of the apostrophe is to indicate possession: *John's bike, the cat's saucer, Wednesday's child*. In fact, it always signifies the omission of a letter or letters. The original form of the possessive was 'John, his bike'. This was contracted to the "'s", which then became applied indiscriminately whether the person or thing concerned was masculine, feminine or neuter. A frequent mistake is the omission of the apostrophe in such phrases as *a year's work* and *a fortnight's holiday*. On the other hand, although strictly we should say, *the baker's* or *Sainsbury's*, because the expressions are short for 'the baker's shop' or 'Sainsbury's shop', there is an increasing tendency to drop the apostrophe in such cases.

Some confusion arises with the possessives of singular words ending in s. They should also take 's: *the Cross's significance, the morass's appearance*. But we usually get round the awkward sound of such possessives by saying, for instance, *the significance of the Cross*, or *the appearance of the morass*. Please note that proper names ending in s also take 's to indicate the possessive case: *Mr Williams's dog, St James's Square, Dickens's books*.

When we want to express the possessive of a plural word ending in s, the apostrophe goes at the end of the word without the addition of an extra s: *Several girls' clothes were lost*, or *the politicians' pay rise*. If the plural ends in -es, it is quite correct to put an apostrophe by itself at the end of the word to indicate the possessive, but again we usually get round the problem by saying, for instance, *the gardens of the houses* rather than *the houses' gardens*. Plurals which do not end in s are given 's: *the women's protest*, or *the mice's tails*.

Apart from possessives, the other main use of the apostrophe is, as already stated, to show that a letter or letters have been dropped. For example: *don't, didn't, wouldn't*. Please note, the form is not *did'nt* or *would'nt*, because in all of those cases the apostrophe stands for the letter o, which has been dropped from 'do not', 'did not', 'would not'. In contractions such as *we'd* or *you'll* or *fo'castle* more than one letter has been dropped, the full form being 'we would' (or 'we had') or 'you will' or 'forecastle'. There are also some rather extraordinary words like *shan't*, which should really appear as *sha'n't* since there have been two separate contractions (of 'shall' and of 'not'), but which is accepted with the single apostrophe, and *won't*, which we say instead of 'will not'.

The dropped letter is of course the reason for the apostrophe in *it's*, meaning 'it is'. *It's* should not be confused with *its*, which is the possessive form of 'it'.

Apostrophes can appear in many places as well as in the middle of words: at the end, for instance, in *huntin', shootin' and fishin'*, or at the beginning, as seen particularly in the reproduction of Cockney speech – *'Ave yer seen 'em?* Or: *'is 'orrible 'ound.* Many new long words that come into the language inevitably get shortened – we say *phone*, for instance, instead of *telephone*, and *bus* for *omnibus*. When such contractions first appear, it is usual to put an apostrophe in front of them, so people used to write *'phone* and *'bus*, but after a while the contractions become so generally used that the apostrophe is dropped.

A further use of the apostrophe is to indicate the plurals of single letters: *Mind your p's and q's*. It used also to be inserted when using the plurals of numbers and abbreviations: *the 1980's, There are three 4's in 12, B.A.'s, G.P.'s*, but nowadays the practice is more often to write, *the 1980s, 4s* and, since it is acceptable also to omit the full stops, *BAs, GPs*.

Quotation Marks

Quotation marks, or inverted commas, indicate direct speech. For example: *'Were you there?' she asked. 'Yes,' he replied. 'Then you must have seen it,' she said.* They are also used to enclose a quotation, or to show that you are using a word with a special, usually popular, meaning: *He pleaded that 'the quality of mercy' might be shown to his client.* Or: *If you like the 'classics', you will probably admire Jane Austen.*

A further use of quotation marks is to enclose a title or name: *The action of 'Hamlet' takes place in Denmark.* Or: *the 'City' class of locomotive.* Or: *Rodin's 'The Kiss'.* It is almost always preferable to use italics in such cases (see below).

Quotation marks normally come in pairs – that is to say, at the beginning of the direct speech or quotation and at its end. However, if a speech by one character or a single quotation consists of more than one paragraph, the convention is to open the quotation marks at the beginning of each paragraph, and to close them only at the end of the last paragraph.

There are two main problems with quotation marks. The first is whether to use single or double quotation marks in your typescript. There is no definite rule. Both are acceptable, but the tendency to choose single inverted commas is increasing. Many publishers have their own 'house rules' on this and other subjects (such as whether the Deity must always be given a capital letter), and will correct your typescript accordingly, or give instructions to the printer to do so. I must say that I prefer to use double quotes in a typescript, because the single quote on a typewriter looks exactly the same as an apostrophe, and that can cause confusion.

When, in dialogue, the speaker quotes the exact words of some other person, or includes a quotation or a word with a special meaning in his speech, the convention is to use single inverted commas for the quoted material if you are normally using double inverted commas, and vice versa. For example: *"Gary said, 'I am going to the shops,' and that was the last I saw of him," he told her.* Or: *'I plead that "the quality of mercy" should be shown to my client.'* Or: *"If you like the 'classics'," he said, "you will probably admire Jane Austen."*

The second difficulty concerns the placing of other punctuation marks when quotation marks are used. Generally speaking, the rule is to put them inside the inverted commas. For instance: *'Where are you going?' she asked.* Not: *'Where are you going'? she asked.* Or: *'I don't know,' he said.* Not: *'I don't know', he said.* (By the way, no extra full stop outside the quotation marks is required when the attribution precedes the line of dialogue: *He turned to her and said, 'I love you.'* Not: *He turned to her and said, 'I love you.'.)* On the other hand, if you are quoting a single word or short phrase, it is often legitimate to put the punctuation outside the inverted commas: *If you admire the 'classics', you will probably admire Jane Austen.* Or: *Invoking 'the quality of mercy', he pleaded for his client.*

The Hyphen

The main function of hyphens is to link together words which have a special meaning when so joined. For instance: *first-night, dog-like, best-seller, dry-clean, sweet-shop.* Other words are traditionally hyphenated, although the meaning is not necessarily at all obscure if there is a space between them, instead of a hyphen, or if they are written as a single word. For example: *first-born, top-class, semi-colon.* Indeed, the modern tendency is to omit the hyphen and put the two words together: *firstnight, doglike, bestseller, semicolon,* and usages like *to-morrow* and *to-day* have virtually disappeared in favour of *tomorrow* and *today.* If you want to use hyphens, you can usually tell whether or not they are necessary by trying the experiment of writing the two words as one. If, for example, you wanted to say *The first night it happened*, it would not be reasonable to write *The firstnight it happened*; on the other hand, if you were referring to *a first-night audience*, it would be possible to use the form *firstnight*, and that is therefore a case in which you have a choice between using a hyphen and running the two words together. There are still some cases where hyphens are essential – *four-year-old houses*, for instance, has an entirely different meaning if the first hyphen is omitted.

Hyphens are also needed in certain phrases which are used almost as single words, but which would look very odd with spaces between their elements, or if run together. For example: *will-o'-the-wisp, devil-may-care, love-in-the-mist* (the flower).

The hyphen is also the conventional sign for a break in a word at the end of a line when there has not been room to complete it. The art of hyphenation in such cases is to break the word in an appropriate place. For instance, if the word 'conventional' were needed to be broken at the end of a line, the best place for the hyphen would be before the t – *conven-tional*, rather than *convent-ional* or, even worse, *conve-ntional*.

Although the hyphen is usually a linking device, in some cases it is used to separate. Thus we write *co-adjudicator*, because *coadjudicator*, by the juxtaposition of the two vowels, makes the word difficult to understand at first sight. *Strap-hanger* is a less obvious example; if you saw it printed as *straphanger*, you would probably have no difficulty with it, but it would nevertheless be possible, at first glance, to pronounce it to yourself as *straffanger*. The hyphen may also be used as a separating device if you want to indicate perhaps that someone saying a long word has deliberately split it into syllables for emphasis: '*It is fund-a-mental!*', or, of course, in an expression such as *abso-bloody-lutely*.

Italics

There are two principal uses of italics: to emphasize a word or words, and to indicate a title (such as that of a literary work, or even, if rarely, that of a public house), or a foreign word (unless, like 'apartheid' or 'aide-de-camp' it has become anglicized). For example: 'He said that when he even *thought* of *the King's Head* he experienced a *frisson*, since it was there that he had first read *The Turn of the Screw*.' Or: 'The direction for the first movement of Mendelssohn's *Italian Symphony* is *allegro vivace*; the conductor took it so slowly that it lasted almost *twice* as long as usual.'

Italics may also be used for a quotation, instead of surrounding the words with inverted commas. For example: 'Hamlet, in the famous soliloquy beginning *To be or not to be*, reveals the indecision in his mind.' They are also a convenient way of separating a specific part of a text from the rest of it, as in the examples of various usages given in this book.

When we are writing by hand, or on a typewriter, we underline any material which, when printed, will appear in italics. If you have a typewriter or a word processor which can produce italics, don't use the facility – underlining will indicate more clearly to the typesetter that he is to set the words concerned in italics.

It is perhaps worth noting that if you wish to emphasize words or show titles in a text the rest of which is in italics, those words will appear in roman (upright) type – for example: *It may be claimed that* Hamlet *is the greatest of Shakespeare's tragedies* – so in your typescript you would leave them without underlining.

Capital Letters

It goes without saying that you need a capital letter at the beginning of a sentence, and this includes the beginning of dialogue, even if it has been preceded by an attribution. For example: *He asked,* 'Where are we going?' A capital is not needed if the attribution comes in the middle of the speech. For example: *'I believe,' he said, 'that it is true.'* Capitals are also used for the names of people, places, organizations, the months and the days of the week, and for titles (for example: *the Prince of Wales*, or *the Leader of the Opposition*). They are also used in certain abbreviations – *UNESCO, MP* – when capitals would be given to the words for which the letters stand (but not in such abbreviations as *a.m.* or *i.e.*). Capitals should also be given to the adjectives derived from the names of countries, such as *English, French*, and *German*.

Don't use capital letters unnecessarily. 'Archbishop', for instance, is a title and is given a capital if you write, say, *the Archbishop conducted the wedding ceremony*. But it is also a common noun, and no capital is needed for it in such a sentence as *the function of an archbishop is to lead the clergy*.

2   Spelling

Spelling used to be taught in schools, and tuition was greatly needed because English spelling is undoubtedly difficult to master. From Victorian times right through to the 1930s 'spelling bees' were popular, in which teams competed against each other in trying to spell correctly anything from the slightly tricky 'separate' (not 'seperate') to real stinkers like 'eschscholtzia'. Nowadays, however, the ability to spell well is often regarded as a mild eccentricity, and many teachers feel that it is far more important to encourage children to express themselves in an interesting way than to bother about whether the words they use are properly spelt or not (and let us face the fact that several of the younger generation of teachers, brought up under the same system, are not so hot at it themselves).

I think this lack of attention to spelling is a pity, and while I agree that a facility with words should be a target for every pupil, I don't see why the children should not be taught simultaneously to get their spelling right.

It is particularly regrettable that so many authors cannot spell. Spelling, punctuation, grammar, and indeed everything to do with words, are the tools of the author's trade, and just as a carpenter will keep his chisels sharpened and his saw slightly greased to prevent rust, so an author should take every possible care with the tools he uses. There is in fact some excuse for those of us who use English. Our grammar is fairly simple, and we have done away with most inflexive endings to words, but we have what is probably the world's most extraordinary spelling, which frequently bears little relation to pronunciation. What other language, for instance, can boast of such confusion as ten different ways of pronouncing that infamous group of four letters, 'ough'?

No one demands perfection. Even the most literate authors sometimes slip up on certain 'bogey' words. I count myself a good speller, but was rightly reprimanded by some reviewers when, in a previous book, after going on about the importance of spelling, I used the word 'miniscule' (it should, of course, have been 'minuscule'). But let your spelling mistakes be few and far between, the exception rather than the rule. A good dictionary is an essential for any writer, and you should never look upon it as a waste of time to check the spelling of any word when you are not absolutely certain of it.

'Why bother at all,' you may ask, 'when publishers employ editors who will correct my spelling?' Partly because a well-presented, well-spelt, well-punctuated typescript really does give you a slight edge when it is considered for publication – the editor thinks, Ah, this is someone who really cares about writing, someone who is taking a more professional approach than most. But you should also take trouble as a matter of your own pride. Why rely on someone else to put you right when you could, with a little trouble, do it for yourself?

It may help you to make your own list of words which you find difficult, so that you can check them quickly. Some of those words may appear in the list which begins on the next page. (Incidentally, a separate note of certain words included not so much for their spelling but for the style in which you are going to use them may also prove worthwhile. Are you, for instance, going to use the form 'bestseller', or will you hyphenate it as 'best-seller'? Are you going to write 'the village hall' or 'the Village Hall'? It is easy to forget which particular mode you have used earlier in your book, and a list will help you to be consistent.)

It really is possible to learn to spell, and it's never too late to start. If you use your list regularly, you will probably find, after a time, that you have learnt the correct spellings and will never again have difficulty with them. That really is the best way of all to learn.

Another way is to read with care and attention. In her excellent book *Becoming a Writer*, Dorothea Brande suggests that you should read a book twice in quick succession: the first time simply to enjoy the story, and the re-reading so as to try to discover how the author tells it, the techniques used, the successes and failures of the narrative. During that second reading, you might also pay attention to the spelling, and attempt to learn from it. (Don't, by the way, rely on newspapers for correct spelling; it is not that journalists can't spell, but that all too often printing errors creep into their columns.)

It is helpful, too, to be careful in your pronunciation, which can often give a guide to the spelling. For instance, if you say the word properly, you will know that it should be 'implicate', not 'implacate' or 'implecate', and you will not write 'refrence' if you say it, correctly, as 'reference'. Of course, this does not always help: we make no difference in the sounds of many words, and not only simple ones like 'made' and 'maid', but also in longer and more easily confused words such as 'complement' and 'compliment'. There is also danger, for example, in the false belief that 'disastrous' should really be pronounced, and spelt, 'disasterous'.

Some Correct Spellings

accelerate (two c's)
accommodation (two c's and two m's)
accordion (not accordeon)
acknowledgment, acknowledgement (either is acceptable)
acoustic (not accoustic)
acquaintance (note the first c)
acquire (note the c)
aerated (not aereated)
affair (no need to add a final e when writing of a romantic liaison)
aggravate (two g's)
agreeable (one g)
align, alignment (not aline, alinement)
allege (not alledge)
all right (preferable to alright)
almighty (only one l)
alms (not arms, in the sense of offerings to the needy)
Alsatian (not Alsation)
aluminium (aluminum is the American spelling)
ambidextrous (not ambidexterous)
appalling (two p's and two l's)
aubrietia
auxiliary (not auxilary)

bachelor (not batchelor)
banister (only one n)
benefited (only one f and one t)
biased (preferable to biassed)
bizarre
bony (not boney)

camellia (two l's)
canvass (the usual spelling when the meaning is to seek political opinions)
capsize (always '-ize', not '-ise')
chaperon (without a final e)
charisma, charismatic
chauffeur (two f's)
cheque (not check, except in America, for a bank draft).
chequer (as in 'chequered flag')
chilblain (one l)
chord (not cord when the meaning is a musical sound)
chronic
clientele

coconut (not cocoanut)
coiffeur (meaning a hairdresser)
coiffure (meaning hairstyle)
colander (only one l, but cullender is also acceptable)
committee (two m's, two t's, two e's)
conscience (note the second c)
conscious (note the second c)
consummate (two m's)
controversy (not contraversy)

delirious (not delerious)
dependant (the noun)
dependent (the adjective)
desiccated (one s, two c's)
deteriorate (note the i)
developed (one p)
diarrhea (or diarrhoea)
dilapidated (not delapidated)
diphtheria (not diptheria)
diphthong (not dipthong)
disappear (one s, two p's)
disappoint (one s, two p's)
disastrous (not disasterous)
discomfit (discomfort is rarely used as a verb)
dullness (two l's)

ecstasy (not ecstacy)
eerie
embarrass (two r's)
excite
exercise (not excercise)
existence (not existance)

fascinate
focusing (only one s)
forbade (pronounced 'forbad')
forgivable (no e after the v)
fulfil, fulfilment (one l)
fulfilled (two l's)
fulsome (one l)

gladioli (not gladiolae – the singular is gladiolus)
gramophone (not gramaphone)
granddaughter (two d's)
grey (gray is the American spelling)
gypsy (preferable to gipsy)

haemorrhage
hallo, hello, hullo (all acceptable, but hillo looks affected)
handful (only one l)

harass (one r)
hereditary (not hereditry)
hiccup (preferable to hiccough)
hirsute (not hersute)
honorary (not honourary or honoury)
humorous (no u after the first o)
hypocrisy (not hypocricy)
hysterical

idiosyncrasy
imaginary (not imaginery)
independent (not independant)
instal, instalment (or install, installment)
installation (two l's)
intercede (not interceed)
irascible
irrelevant (not irelevant or irrevelant)
itinerary (not itinery)

jewellery (preferable to jewelry, which is the American spelling)
judgment, judgement (either is acceptable)

ketchup (preferable to catsup)
kidnapped (two p's – kidnaped is the American spelling)

lachrymose
lacquer
lightning (as in 'thunder and lightning', not lightening)
liquefy (not liquify)
liqueur (not licqueur)
liquor (not licquor)
liquorice (not licquorice or liquorish)

macabre
mackintosh (don't forget the k)
maintenance (not maintainance)
manoeuvre (maneuver is the American spelling)
mantelpiece (not mantlepiece)
matt (meaning dull in finish, not mat)
mediaeval, medieval (either is acceptable)
mien
millepede (preferable to millipede)
minuscule (not miniscule)
mischievous (not mischievious)
mistakable (not mistakeable)
monstrous (not monsterous)
mouth (not mouthe when used as a verb as in 'to mouth the words')

naphtha (not naptha)
necessary (one c, two s's)
noticeable (not noticable)

nuclear (not neuclear)

obeisance
obscene
opportunity (not oppertunity)
orang-utan (or, less usually, orang-outang)

pallor (not pallour)
paraffin (two f's)
parallel (not paralell or paralel)
parliament (note the second a)
persistent (not persistant)
phenomenon (not phenomenom)
possess ('possess possesses many esses')
prejudice (not predjudice)
privilege (not priviledge or privelege)
proffer (two f's)
putrefy (not putrify)

questionnaire (two n's)

racquet (as in 'tennis racquet')
reconnoitre (one c, two n's)
recuperate (not recouperate)
relevant (not revelant)
renege (not renaig, but renegue is also used)
rhetorical
rhyme
rhythm
rigor (as in *'rigor mortis'*)
rigour (meaning 'severity')

saccharin (the sweetener)
saccharine (meaning 'over-sweet')
sacrilegious (not sacreligious)
sceptic, sceptical (not skeptic, skeptical, which is American usage)
sceptre (note the c)
schedule (not shedule or skedule)
secateurs (one c)
secretary (not secertary)
separate (not seperate)
sepulchre
silhouette
sillabub (or syllabub)
skilful (single l's both times)
slyly (not slily)
sobriquet (not soubriquet)
somersault (not somersalt)
speciality (specialty is an American usage)
spectator (not spectater)

spurt (spirt is also acceptable)
squalor (not squalour)
storey, storeyed (referring to the floors of a building)
strait-jacket (not straight-jacket)
stupefy (not stupify)
success (two c's and two s's at the end)
sumptuous (not sumptious)
supersede (not supercede)
surprise (not surprize)
surveillance
susceptible
synchronize (not sinchronise)
synthetic (not sinthetic)

temporary (not tempory)
titillate (two l's)
tranquil (one l)
tranquillity (two l's)
tremor (not tremour)
tyro (tiro is also acceptable)

umbrella (not umberella)
unconscious
unnecessary (two n's as well as two s's)

vermilion (one l)
veterinary (not vetinary)
vigorous (not vigourous)

waiver (the relinquishing of a right)
waver (meaning 'one who waves' or 'to hesitate' or 'to flicker')
whiskey (the Irish form)
whisky (Scotch)
wilful (not willful)
wistaria (not wisteria)
withhold (two h's)
woollen (not woolen)
wryly (not wrily)

It should be noted that some of the spellings above may vary in American usage. Reference should also be made to the list of common problem words on pages 69-88.

Rules for Spelling

English, as I have said, is not an easy language to spell correctly, and although certain basic rules exist, they are often complex and riddled with exceptions. Take, for instance, the familiar saying, 'i before e, except after c'. It sounds very simple, but the first thing to remember is that it applies principally when the syllable concerned has an 'ee' sound, as in 'deceive' or 'receipt' (after c), or 'yield' or 'hygienic' (following a letter other than c). It is not an entirely reliable rule, because of such exceptions as 'species' and 'seize', 'seizure', 'counterfeit', 'weir', 'weird' and certain chemical words like 'caffeine' or 'codeine', despite the fact that all of these have the 'ee' sound. When the sound is not 'ee', the e usually comes before the i, as in 'deign', 'reign', 'heir' or 'leisure' (you may,by the way, get thoroughly mixed up about 'leisure' if you use the American pronunication 'leesure'). And again there are exceptions, such as 'friend'. It is all very confusing. Nevertheless, if you follow the rule 'i before e, except after c (when the sound is ee)', you will be right more often than wrong.

All the rules of English spelling, together with lists of exceptions, can be found in any good English Grammar, or in such a useful book as *The Oxford Guide to the English Language*, which also includes a dictionary containing some 30,000 words. Another extremely valuable book is *Hart's Rules for Compositors and Readers at the University Press, Oxford*. First produced in 1893 by Harold Hart, who was Printer to the University, and originally intended solely for the use of printers, it has been revised and updated since, and has become indispensable to many authors as well as to printers. It gives a great deal of information on spelling (and on a variety of other subjects), including, for instance: lists of those words which end in -able and those which end in -ible (such as 'excitable' and 'extendible' – it is an interesting fact, by the way, that -able is a far more common ending than -ible); difficult and unusual plurals (such as 'ghettos', 'mottoes', 'poets laureate'); words which double their final letter when a suffix like -ing is added (for instance, 'refer' and 'referring'), etc.

Anyone who has difficulty with spelling will find it worth while to buy the *Oxford Guide* or *Hart's Rules*. However, one word of caution should be added: there are a few cases when the spelling which they recommend may be regarded as something of a personal choice of the Oxford University Press. For instance, both books suggest strongly that you should always use -ize rather than -ise in such words as 'realize', 'criticize', 'civilize' (but not in certain others including 'televise', 'exercise', 'surprise'). However, the use of the -ise ending is becoming far more acceptable than the Oxford books would suggest, and you will not be wrong if you use them. In any case, you may find that your publisher has strong feelings on this particular question (and on such matters as the use of capital letters, and whether or not there should always be a full stop after Dr, Mr,

Mrs and Ms). If the publisher has such firm house rules, he will not condemn you for not following them, but will make suitable alterations in your typescript before it is sent to the printer.

The Really Hopeless Speller

I recognize, of course, that there are some writers who have a block about spelling, amounting to near dyslexia. If you are such an author, don't rely on the publisher to correct your work. There are two possible courses of action open to you. The first is to look up in a dictionary every word you write; this is a laborious process, made worse since you will probably be looking the word up the way you think it's spelt and may not be able to find it as a result; all you can do in that case is to check every possible spelling until you find the right one.

The following list of sounds which may have confusing spellings may help:

A Phonetic Guide

Sound	*Possible unexpected spellings*	
a (as in 'day')	a–e	(male, militate)
	ae	(Gaelic)
	ai	(bait, laid)
	ao	(gaol)
	au	(gauge)
	ay	(day, stray)
	e or é	(usually in foreign words, such as auto-da-fé, fiancé)
	ea	(break, steak)
	ei	(deign, weight)
	ey	(prey, they)
a (as in 'mat')	ai	(plaid)
a (as in 'father')	ae	(heart)
	al	(calf, half)
	au	(laugh)
	er	(clerk, sergeant)
b	bb	(bubble, stubble)
c (as in 'cat')	cc	(accuse, occupy)
	ch	(cholera, chronicle)
	ck	(sack, tickle)
	k	(kaleidoscope, king)
	kh	(khaki)
	qu	(liquor)
	que	(physique, unique)
ch	t	(future, question)

Sound		*Possible unexpected spellings*
	tch	(match, ratchet)
cw	ch	(choir)
	qu	(question, quick)
d	dd	(griddle, muddle)
	ld	(could, would)
e (as in 'see')	ae	(aesthete)
	ay	(quay)
	ea	(leak, pea)
	e–e	(sere, theme)
	ee	(committee, see)
	ei	(seize, weir)
	eo	(people)
	ey	(key)
	i	(police)
	ie	(families, wield)
e (as in 'bed')	a	(any, many)
	ae	(anaesthetic)
	ai	(said)
	ay	(says)
	ea	(dead, treasure)
	ei	(leisure)
	eo	(jeopardy)
	ie	(friend)
f	ff	(sniffle, suffer)
	ft	(soften)
	gh	(laugh, rough)
	ph	(philanthrophy, physical)
g (as in 'girl')	gg	(giggle, struggle)
	gh	(ghastly, ghetto)
	gu	(guess, guide)
g (as in 'gentle')	dg	(ledge, midget)
	dj	(adjoin, adjutant)
	gg	(exaggerate)
	j	(jewel, jury)
h	wh	(who)
i (as in 'like')	ai	(aisle)
	ei	(height)
	ie	(fie, lied)
	i–e	(file, rite)
	y	(fry, spy)
i (as in 'bit')	ie	(sieve)
	o	(women)
	u	(business)
	y	(rhythm, sympathy)
j	dg	(edgy, lodge)
	dj	(adjudicator, adjust)
	g	(gesture, gin)
	gg	(exaggerate)
k	c	(cataract, comic)

Sound	Possible unexpected spellings	
	cc	(acclaim, ecclesiastic)
k	ch	(chromium, scholar)
	ck	(pocket, track)
	kh	(khaki)
	qu	(liquorice)
	que	(pique, toque)
kw	ch	(choir)
	qu	(quantity, quota)
l	ll	(llama, pull)
m	mb	(comb, dumb)
	mm	(dimmer, summer)
	mn	(hymn, solemn)
n	gn	(gnome, gnu)
	kn	(knife, knowledge)
	nn	(running, winner)
	pn	(pneumatic)
o (as in 'low')	au	(mauve)
	eau	(bureau, trousseau)
	eo	(yeoman)
	ew	(sew)
	oa	(broach, load)
	oe	(ice-floe, potatoes)
	oo	(brooch)
	ou	(dough, soul)
	ow	(crow, follow)
o (as in 'top')	a	(quantity, watch)
	ou	(cough)
o (as in 'or')	au	(maul, taut)
	aw	(flaw, saw)
	oo	(floor)
	ou	(ought, thought)
ow	ou	(our, plough)
p	pp	(copper, ripple)
r	rh	(rheumatism, rhododendron)
	rr	(curry, mirror)
	wr	(wretch, writer)
s	c	(centre, cistern)
	ce	(ice, licence)
	ps	(psalm, psychology)
	sc	(ascend, science)
	ss	(asset, bass)
	st	(castle, fastened)
	sw	(sword)
sh	c	(ocean, special)
	ch	(chaperon, machine)
	s	(mansion, sugar)
	sc	(conscious)
	ss	(fission, session)

Sound	Possible unexpected spellings	
	t	(action, conventional)
	x	(anxious)
t	bt	(debt, redoubt)
	ct	(indict)
	ed	(forked, talked)
	pt	(ptomaine, receipt)
	th	(thyme)
	tt	(battle, sitting)
u (as in 'mud')	o	(done, ton)
	oo	(bloody)
	ou	(double, younger)
u (as in 'cute')	eau	(beauty)
	eu	(pneumonia, pseudo)
	ew	(lewd, new)
	o–e	(move, prove)
	oe	(shoe)
	oo	(food, too)
	ou	(soup, through)
	ue	(flue, true)
	ui	(fruit)
u (as in 'curt')	ea	(heard)
	e	(herd, infer)
	eu	(coiffeur, restaurateur)
	i	(firmament, sir)
	o	(word)
	ou	(journal)
	y	(myrrh)
x	cs	(ecstasy, tocsin)
	ct	(fiction, section)
z	s	(cosy, freesia)
	ss	(scissors)
	x	(xylophone)
	zz	(dazzle, jazz)
zh	s	(casual, treasure)

In the above list there are some examples of silent letters, such as the p in 'ptomaine'. Other silent letters which often occur are h, in words like 'heir' and 'hour', and s in 'isle' and 'island'.

It will always help you to find words in a dictionary if you pronounce them carefully, sounding the d in 'soldier', for instance, as a d rather than 'dg'.

The easier alternative to looking up everything in a dictionary is to seek help from a friend who can spell. You must surely know *someone* who is good at spelling and who would be willing – indeed, may be flattered to be asked – to correct your work before you type out the fair copy.

3 Grammar

Grammar is concerned with the parts of speech and the formation of sentences and clauses. It is a subject which can occupy whole books and to which teachers used to devote many hours of instruction. For the average person it is not a subject of immense interest, but anyone who wants to write well is, or should be, a lover of words and everything to do with them, and grammar is the basis on which we put words together for the purposes of communication.

I once asked a class to write a short piece without using adjectives or adverbs, and one of my pupils had to confess that she did not know what an adverb was. If you are like that lady, this chapter is essential reading for you, and if you want to know more than the rudiments, there are many good books easily available. If you already have a good grounding in grammar, you will probably not mind reading about it again.

Parts of Speech

Parts of speech are the names we give to words when they are performing various functions – as names, perhaps, or action words, or to describe or modify other words, or to define their relationships to each other. It is often impossible to know in which function a particular word is operating until it appears in a sentence. The word *love*, for instance, can be a noun (*my love of books*), a verb (*I love you*) or an adjective (as in *love story*); *like* can be a verb (*he likes strawberries*), an adjective (*the falcon, and like predators*), an adverb (*she moved like lightning*) or even a noun (*roses, dahlias and the like*); while the present participle of a verb can be a noun (*parting is such sweet sorrow*), an adverb (*he came running*) or an adjective (*typing paper*).

THE NOUN

A noun is the name of something, and the majority are known as 'common' nouns (for example: *dog, table, grain, office, rubbish,* etc.). A 'proper' noun (always given a capital letter, unless you are a disciple of the American writer e.e.cummings) is the name of a person, a town, a country, etc. (for example: *Jennifer, Middlesbrough, France, Monday, the Iron Duke*).

Nouns can be singular (*song, bird, keg*) or plural (*songs, birds, kegs*). The plural form is usually indicated simply by adding an s, but there are many, mostly familiar, irregular plurals, such as *mouse* and *mice, ox* and *oxen, knife* and *knives,* while nouns which end in -ch, -s, -sh and -x take -es (*match* and *matches, mass* and *masses, sash* and *sashes, box* and *boxes*). Other exceptions are nouns ending in a consonant followed by y, which change the -y into -ies (*ruby* and *rubies, caddy* and *caddies*); but note that if the y is preceded by a vowel, the plural is formed simply by adding s, (*boy* and *boys, ray* and *rays*), a point which would hardly be worth making if it were not for the mistake commonly made with *money,* the plural of which is *moneys,* not *monies.*

The formation and use of plurals is simple enough to most of us until we come to 'collective' nouns – words such as *crowd, police, school, people.* Although made up of several elements, a crowd or a school is a single entity and should therefore take a singular verb and a singular pronoun – *The crowd is hostile, and it looks quite frightening.* Or: *The whole school gathers in its main hall each morning.* But some collective nouns, like *police* and *people* always take plural verbs – *The police want to question him in the course of their enquiries.* Or: *The people demand an answer; they are in no mood for shilly-shallying.* Most of us know without thinking whether to use a singular or a plural verb or pronoun, but a problem arises with a phrase like *a crowd of hooligans,* or *a school of porpoises. Crowd* and *school* are the governing words in those cases, and we should really say *A crowd of hooligans is coming this way,* or *A school of porpoises frolics in the water*; it seems much more natural, however, because the plural noun intervenes before the verb, to say *A crowd of hooligans are coming this way,* or *A school of porpoises frolic in the water.* Either is acceptable nowadays, at least in speech, but it is preferable to use the correct verb in writing. And always beware of mixing plurals and singulars in one sentence, like a news broadcast heard recently: *The government have announced its plans ... Government* is a collective noun, when used in this way, and can take either a singular or a plural verb and pronoun, but not both in one sentence.

Although, except for genitives, the form of the word does not change, nouns have four cases:

The nominative, when the noun is the subject of a sentence (*The river runs swiftly, The bibliophile smiled* – *The river* and *The bibliophile* being the subjects).

The accusative, when the noun is the direct object in a sentence (*The boy reads the book, The woman washed the dress* – *The boy* and *The woman* being the subjects, and *the book* and *the dress* being the objects).

The dative, when the noun is the indirect object in a sentence (*John gave the present to Julia, The foreman told the workmen what he had said* – *John* and *The foreman* being the subjects, *the present* and *what he had said* being the direct objects, and *Julia* and *the workmen* being the indirect objects).

The genitive, which indicates that the noun or pronoun owns or is the source of something (*That ball is the dog's, the boys' uniforms, the countryside of England, Jesus's teachings* – *dog's, boys', of England* and *Jesus's* are all genitives). The genitive is usually indicated by an apostrophe (with or without an s) or by 'of'.

THE PRONOUN

Pronouns are words which takes the place of a noun or nouns, and there are many varieties of them.

First, there are the personal pronouns, which take five different forms:

The nominative – *I, thou, he, she, it, we, you, they*.

The accusative (also used for the dative) – *me, thee, him, her, it, us, you, them*.

The possessive (or genitive) – *mine, thine, his, hers, its* (N.B. not *it's*, which is short for *it is*), *ours, yours, theirs*. (Please note that *ours, yours* and *theirs* do not use apostrophes.) These pronouns are not to be confused with *my, thy, his, her, our, your, their*, which are adjectives rather than pronouns.

The reflexive and emphatic, which both use the same words – *myself, thyself, ourselves*, etc. The difference between reflexive and emphatic can be seen in such sentences as *He killed himself* (reflexive), or *I myself was there* (emphatic).

The principal problem with personal pronouns arises in such a phrase as *you and I*. Because people are aware that it is wrong to say, for example, *You and me will go*, instead of *You and I will go*, they tend always to use the nominative pronouns when often they should not. *Between you and I and the gate-post*, or *He wanted you and I to go* are incorrect. *Between* and *wanted* both take the accusative form, and you should therefore say *Between you and me and the gate-post*, or *He wanted you and me to go*. If you leave out the *you and* in such phrases, you will usually see that *I* is wrong: you would probably not say *Between I and the gate-post* or *He told I to go*. (Incidentally, it is worth noting that the real reason for the confusion is that *you* can be either nominative or accusative or dative.)

Next, there are the demonstrative pronouns: *this, that, these, those,* which are pronouns in such sentences as *That is my house, This is Your Life*, or *Those who are about to die salute you*. If, on the other hand, you say *That book belongs to him*, or *These ducklings are two days old*, you are using *that* or *these* as adjectives.

We come next to interrogative and relative pronouns: *who, whom, whose, what, which, that*. They are interrogative when used in direct or indirect questions – *Who is that?* or *She asked which it was* – and relative in such examples as *the sun whose rays are all ablaze* or *the man to whom she spoke* or *What I said was* ... The most confusing of these is *whom*. It is correct to say, for example, *The man whom the Police accused of the crime*, but *whom* is wrong in such a sentence as *The man whom it is said is already known to the Police was arrested*. If we put in the necessary commas – *The man, whom, it is said, is known to the Police, was arrested*, we can see that *it is said* is an interpolation in the clause which at present reads *whom is known to the police*. Leave out the interpolation, and it becomes clear that the clause should be *who is known to the police*.

Finally, there is a large group of indefinite pronouns, which include:

The impersonal pronouns – *one, you, they* – as in such usages as *One does one's best, You always hurt the one you love, They say a stitch in time saves nine*.

The distributive pronouns (when these words are used by themselves rather than as adjectives) – *some, all, any, many, none, several, both, much, each, either, neither, few* (and *fewer* and *fewest*), *more* (and *most*), *former, latter, such*, and the words formed by the addition of *-one, -body*, and *-thing* to *any, every, no* and *some*, such as *anyone, everybody, nothing, someone*.

THE VERB
Verbs are action words, the words which indicate what the subject of a sentence is doing. They have five basic forms: the infinitive (*to go*), the present (*I go, he goes, we go*), the past (*she went, you went*), the present participle (*going*), the past participle (*gone*).

Two verbs, *to be* and *to have*, although they have their own specific meanings of *to exist* and *to possess*, are also known as 'auxiliary verbs' because they are used in conjunction with certain other verbs to form tenses (see below). Other auxiliaries are *shall, will, may, should, would* and *might* (but only when they are used to form tenses or moods – not when they are 'modals', as indicated below). The verb *to do* is also used in a similar way in such questions or statements as *Do you like reading?* or *I did tell the truth*. The verbs used in conjunction with auxiliaries (*like* and *tell* in the examples just given) are in the infinitive form, although they usually omit the *to*.

Most verbs can stand on their own, but there are some which are used only in combination with other verbs, and are called 'modals': *can, may, might, must, ought, will, shall, would, should, could, let*. These verbs all express the ability or the wish or the obligation to do something, rather than being used as auxiliaries to indicate tenses. Other modals are *dare, need* and *used to*.

Verbs have tenses, which indicate the time at which the action is taking place or has taken place or will take place. The tenses are the present (*I write*), the present imperfect (*I am writing* – formed by the present of the auxiliary *to be* and the present participle of the main verb), the past (*I wrote*), the past imperfect (*I was writing* – formed by the past of the auxiliary *to be* and the past participle), the past perfect (*I have written* – formed by the present of the auxiliary *to have* and the past participle), the pluperfect (*I had written* – formed by the past of the auxiliary *to have* and the past participle), the future (*I shall write, you will write* – formed with the auxiliaries *shall* or *will*), the future-in-the-past (*we should have written, they would have written* – formed with the auxiliaries *should* or *would*). Note that the future takes *shall* for the first person (*I shall write, we shall write*) and *will* for the second and third persons (*you will write, they will write*); if *will* is used for the first person, and *shall* for the second and third persons, they become modals and the sense changes from the simple future of the verb to one of determination or obligation.

There are other ways of expressing the future or the future-in-the-past: by the use of the auxiliary *to be* and *going* (*I am going to write, you were going to write*); by the use of the auxiliary *to be* with the infinitive of the verb (*We are to write to him tomorrow*) or with the present participle of the verb (*They are writing to him tomorrow*); by the use of the present tense together with a word or phrase which in itself expresses the future (*I write to him next week*).

Verbs have two voices: active (*Sue drove the car*) and passive (*The car was driven by Sue*).

Verbs have four moods: the indicative, used in straightforward statements or questions (*The sky is blue, Who goes home?*); the imperative, used in commands (*Go away, Don't do that*); the subjunctive, used in the expression of possibility, uncertainty or hope (*if I were you, He suggested that the meeting be adjourned, May you be very happy, had he known the outcome, They would join in, if they could*); and the infinitive, often preceded by *to*, in which form it may be simple (*to make, to sing*), or modified by forms of the verbs *to be* or *to have* (*to be going, to have gone*).

Verbs can be transitive or intransitive. Transitive verbs are those which take a direct object (*He chopped the wood, Jan gave up smoking*). Intransitive verbs do not take a direct object, and are frequently concerned with movement (*to come, to go, to appear*). Some normally intransitive verbs are sometimes forced into becoming transitive; the verb *to smile*, for instance, is usually intransitive, but it is possible to say something like, *The leprechaun smiled a funny, mocking smile*, and in that sentence the verb has become transitive.

THE ADVERB

An adverb is a word which is attached to a verb, an adjective, a preposition or another adverb to indicate manner, degree, time or place. For example: *She smiled sadly. The monster was undoubtedly dead. He told her later. He parked close by Rupert's two-seater..*

Adverbs can consist of single words (*sadly, undoubtedly, later, close* in the above examples are all adverbs) or of phrases. For example: *She smiled in a sad way. The monster was without question dead. He told her at two o'clock. He parked with inches to spare by Rupert's two-seater.*

A special kind of adverb is the 'conjunctive adverb', used to link two sentences. These include words and phrases such as *however, on the other hand, especially, in conclusion*.

Many adverbs are formed by adding -ly or -ally to an adjective (*slowly, beautifully, prosaically*), but others, such as *hard, fast, late* and *early* (and their comparative forms, *harder, hardest*, etc.) do not change the adjectival form. *Deep* can be used either as an adjective or an adverb, but one can also add -ly to make the adverb *deeply*.

THE ADJECTIVE

An adjective is a descriptive word applied to a noun. Such words as *quick, brown, lazy, descriptive* are adjectives plain and simple.

Other forms are the possessive adjectives (*my, thy, his, her, its, our, your, their*), the demonstrative adjectives (*this, that, these, those*), the interrogative adjectives (*what, whose, which*) and the distributive adjectives (*some, all, any, many, no, several, both, much, each, either, neither, few, fewer, fewest, more, most, former, latter*). You will note that most of these words have already been listed under pronouns. If you say *His won the prize* or *Those were the alternatives* or *Few agreed* or *Either is acceptable* or *Such was the burden of his speech,* you are using *his, those, few, either* and *such* as pronouns; if you say *His essay won the prize* or *Those proposals were the alternatives* or *Few people agreed* or *Either solution is acceptable* or *Such nonsense was the burden of his speech,* you are using them as adjectives.

THE ARTICLE
The, a and *an* are articles, *the* being the definite article and *a* and *an* indefinite articles.

THE PREPOSITION
Prepositions are words such as *to, from, by, with, in, on,* which link a noun with another part of speech to indicate a relationship between them. Some combinations of prepositions have become single words, such as *upon* and *into,* but others remain separated even when used together – *on to* and *up to,* for example.

Prepositions are sometimes used in combination with verbs to form 'phrasal verbs', which have their own special meanings. For example: *break in, get on with, climb down.*

THE CONJUNCTION
Conjunctions are words which link two words, phrases, sentences or clauses. *And, but, either … or* and *neither … nor* are co-ordinating conjunctions since they join words or groups of words of equal importance. The subordinating conjunctions, *unless, as, since, because, if, provided, in order to* and many similar words and phrases are used only to join sentences or clauses of lesser importance to the main statement.

THE INTERJECTION
Interjections are words or short phrases, usually used only in dialogue, indicating an emotional reaction. For example: *Oh, Heavens above, Never, Well, Good Lord, My God* and such splendid old-fashioned expressions as *Pshaw, Ugh* or *'Zounds.* They often stand on their own, with an exclamation mark to emphasize them or a question mark to indicate a querying expression, but can also appear, less emphatically, as the

introduction to a sentence or phrase – *Well, I did so. Oh, I don't think so. Good heavens, no.*

Sentence Structure

A basic sentence is made up of a subject and a predicate (which must include a verb). The subject is the person or thing which performs the action described in the predicate (or, in the passive voice, to whom or on whom the action is performed). The sentence can be as short as two words: we could, for instance, take the pronoun *she* as the subject and the verb *sang* as the predicate, and put them together to produce a complete sentence – *She sang.* Or we can write a much more lengthy sentence, such as the first one in this paragraph, in which *a basic sentence* is the subject, and all the rest is the predicate.

A more elaborate form is to join two sentences into one by the use of a conjunction. For example: *She sang, and the audience applauded.* Or: *A basic sentence is made up of a subject and a predicate, and the latter must always include a verb.*

In addition to the verb, a simple predicate may include a direct object (*She sang the song* – *the song* being the direct object), or an indirect object (*She sang to me* – *to me* being an indirect object), or both a direct and an indirect object (*She sang me the song* – *me* being the indirect object and the song the direct object), and an adverb (*She sang me the song softly* – *softly* being the adverb). Or the predicate may include a complement, the term given to words which follow verbs concerned with existence, such as *to be, to appear, to feel*, and with creation, such as *to make, to appoint*. In the sentences *She is angry* and *He made her angry, angry* is a complement.

CLAUSES
Sentences may also include clauses, in which case they become known as 'complex'. A clause is, in effect, a subordinate sentence, and always includes a verb. It can be adjectival or adverbial – *The cat, which had grown fat since I last saw it, or so it seemed, was sitting by the fire as I entered the room I remembered so well.* That sentence has a long and involved predicate containing five clauses: *which had grown fat* is adjectival, describing the cat; *since I last saw it* is adverbial, qualifying *grown fat*; *or so it seemed* is adverbial, linked to the previous clause by the subordinating conjunction *or*, and further qualifying *grown fat*; *as I entered the*

room is adverbial, indicating when the cat was sitting by the fire; *I remembered so well* (*which*, having been omitted at the beginning of the clause, is nevertheless to be understood) is adjectival, describing the room.

Clauses may be generally distinguished from phrases by the fact that they contain verbs, whereas phrases do not. In *The cat, old and fat, sat by the fire*, the words *old and fat* form an adjectival phrase, although it would turn into a clause if we inserted the understood words *which was*. Some groups of words which contain verbs may still be categorized as phrases – *so to speak*, for example.

Figures of Speech

Certain literary devices are known as 'figures of speech'. We frequently use them in everyday life, without necessarily realizing that we are doing so, and probably in ignorance of the names for them, many of which are unfamiliar and often derived from Greek or Latin. It is certainly not essential for any writer to know those names and to be able to say, 'Ah, that's *zeugma*,' or 'He's used *litotes*.' Nevertheless, in case you do want to use them, or are faced with a creative-writing tutor who talks about them to your bafflement, here is a list of the commoner figures of speech:

ALLEGORY
An allegory is a work which the reader is intended to understand as referring to persons or events other than those directly described. It has similarities with a parable. The author of an allegory usually desires to instruct or to criticize, and uses this device to add to the reader's entertainment and to point his moral more sharply. George Orwell's *Animal Farm* is an allegory which attacks the Stalinist form of Communism.

ALLITERATION
In alliteration two or more words beginning with the same letter are placed next to each other or so close that the similarity of sound is apparent, as in *Round and round the rugged rock the ragged rascal ran*. Alliteration was much used in Old and Middle English poetry.

ANTITHESIS
Antithesis is the setting against each other of contrasting words or ideas. *Two's company, three's a crowd. To lose one parent, Mr Worthing, may be regarded as a misfortune; to lose both looks like carelessness.*

APOSTROPHE

Apostrophe as a figure of speech (not to be confused with the punctuation mark) is seen when a writer or speaker breaks off from what he is saying or writing to address directly a person or thing. For example: *... and then the soldiers came – O God, have mercy on us! – and the looting and the raping and the killings began.* Or, *I loved the view from my bedroom window. O, you meadows and hills, have you now vanished beneath some soulless housing estate?*

BATHOS

Bathos is an anti-climax. Often used for humorous purposes, it usually consists of ending a list of some kind with a triviality, as in *The burglar got away with two thousand pounds in cash, several pieces of valuable jewellery and two packets of Corn Flakes.*

CLIMAX

The opposite of bathos, exemplified in a list in which the items are of ascending importance. *The evening began quietly, became rowdier and ended in a full-scale punch-up.*

EUPHEMISM

Euphemism is the use of a milder expression in place of something unpleasant or something which might appear indelicate. For example: *pass away* instead of *die, powder-room* in place of *lavatory, social disease* instead of *venereal disease.*

EUPHUISM

A name taken from *Euphues*, a book by John Lyly, and used to describe very elaborate, flowery language.

HYPALLAGE

In hypallage a description of one thing is transferred to another to which it does not really belong, as in *a cloudless moon* (it is the sky which is cloudless) or *He is always readable* (his writings are readable).

HYPERBOLE

Hyperbole is a deliberate exaggeration which is recognizable as such. *There are millions of reasons why I can't do it. She puts at least two pounds of grease on her face before she goes to bed. He's so fat that once round his waist is twice round the Albert Hall.*

IRONY

Irony is one of the most familiar figures of speech. It consists of the use of words to convey the very opposite of their natural meaning. *Charming!* we say ironically when someone has behaved outrageously towards us. *Of course, the Minister would never stoop to vote-catching,* says an opposition spokesman with heavy irony, when about to accuse the Minister of that and worse.

LITOTES

Litotes is an understatement. *You might call it slightly cold today* (when the temperature is well below freezing). It is often used with a negative, as in *He's not bad at maths* (meaning that he is pretty good at it).

MALAPROPISM

The absurd misuse of words. The word comes from Mrs Malaprop, a character in Sheridan's *The Rivals,* who was given to such phrases as *an allegory on the banks of the Nile* and *a nice derangement of epitaphs.* She meant, of course, *an alligator* and *arrangement of epithets.*

METAPHOR

In a metaphor the quality or appearance or properties of one thing are attributed to another with which the first has no direct similarity. Another way of explaining it might be to say that a metaphor expresses an idea which is not to be taken literally, but which, by association, paints a vivid picture of what is meant. If we say after a line of dialogue, *he thundered,* we do not mean that he brought about rumblings in the heavens, but that the sound of his voice was like thunder. A comparison is therefore made, but it is an indirect one. Many metaphors have become clichés, such as *a hive of industry* (the metaphor taken from bees) or *at death's door* (the metaphor representing Death as a house-owner).

METONYMY

Metonymy is the use of part of something, or something associated with it, to represent the thing itself. *He took to the bottle* (*the bottle* being substituted for *drinking*). *The way of the Cross* (*Cross* standing for *Christianity*).

ONOMATOPOEIA

The use of words which convey the sound of the object described. *Peewit* is an onomatopoeic name taken from the sound of the bird's call. *The ringing, clanging, jangling sound of the bells* is another example.

OXYMORON
In oxymoron two contrasting ideas are placed together for effect, as in *He said, with smiling despair, that he was never satisfied,* or *the painful pleasure of divorce.*

PARADOX
A statement which appears to be absurd, but which may contain a truth. For example: *Only in death is there life eternal,* or *If you want something done quickly, ask a busy person.*

PERSONIFICATION
Personification is the attribution of human qualities, feelings or actions to non-human objects. For example: *The tree lifts her leafy arms to pray,* or *The sun smiled down upon them,* or *Panic wrapped its icy fingers around her heart.*

PLEONASM
The use of unnecessary words to express an idea, as in *at this point in time* (meaning *now*). *As, as to,* and *of* are also often inserted without good reason, in phrases like *as yet, as to whether and inside of* – *yet, whether* and *inside* are all quite adequate by themselves. A pleonasm is often directly tautological (that is to say, it says the same thing twice in different words, as in *He ambled along, walking slowly.*

PUN
A pun is a play on words in which two different meanings suggest themselves. *His express wish was to come by fast train.* The poet Thomas Hood specialized in puns: *They went and told the sexton, and/The sexton toll'd the bell.*

SIMILE
A simile is a simple comparison, and almost always involves the use of either *as* or *like*. For example: *The ballet dancer seemed as light as thistledown. Like a diamond in the sky.* Many similes have become clichés: *As busy as a bee. He went like lightning. As good as gold.*

SYLLEPSIS
Syllepsis is a figure in which one word is used in two different

senses. *She took her leave and my umbrella,* or *He played the piano and the stock market.* See Zeugma below.

SYNECDOCHE

More or less the opposite of metonymy, synecdoche is the use of the whole to represent the part, as when we say, *The NUM threatened a strike*, when we mean, in fact, that the leaders of the NUM made the threat. Or *Australia won the Test Match*, meaning the Australian team.

ZEUGMA

Zeugma is often used as synonymous with syllepsis, that is to say, a device in which one word is used with two different meanings. Purists draw a distinction between the two figures, saying that in zeugma the word concerned is appropriate to only one of the objects concerned. For example: *Her eyes flashed and frowned her disapproval* (eyes can flash, but cannot frown).

4 Style

For some beginners style is a mystic word, signifying some mysterious quality which can only be achieved after years of practice. But every writer has a style as soon as he or she puts pen to paper, or taps out words on a typewriter or word processor. Style is simply the way you write. The question is, of course, whether you have what is called a good style. How do you decide whether or not your style is good? It may be a matter of personal taste, and it is difficult to make any more definite pronouncement than to say that it should be suitable for the work you want to do. In most cases, the less obtrusive the style, the better it is – if the reader is over-conscious of the way something is written, its style is probably getting in the way of the communication which the author wants to establish with that reader.

If you are fortunate, you will have a good natural style which is also flexible, changing according to the kind of writing you are engaged on. It will probably be unobtrusive, and the reader will be more interested in what you have to say than in the way you say it; he or she will not be distracted by poor syntax, or misused words, or clumsy constructions, or lack of clarity, and equally will not spend so much time admiring the 'beautiful' writing that the actual meaning becomes of secondary importance.

If you do not have this gift, there is no need for despair. It is quite possible to improve your style, provided that you are prepared to accept the idea that writing is a craft which needs to be learnt, practised and constantly looked at with an analytical and self-critical eye. The effort involved is really not over-demanding, and you should be spurred on by the knowledge that even those with an instinctive ability for expressing themselves will, if they are serious about writing, keep refining and polishing their style, trying to reach a higher standard. Only a genius can afford to rest on his or her laurels (and, in fact, few geniuses have ever been content to do so).

51

Let us look at some of the guidelines which you may find worth following.

Write As You Speak

The most common form of human communication is speech. Most of us can talk reasonably fluently, especially when we have something we want to tell other people about. The easiest way to write is to transcribe the words that you would use if you were telling the story or the facts orally, but, just as in a conversation you would try to avoid waffling on with a string of repetitions, hesitations and deviations, it is essential to work out in advance exactly what you want to say. If you know what you are aiming at, your spoken version will probably be direct and to the point; in other words, the style will be good. You may meet some problems. To begin with, our speech is often slovenly, filled with repetitions, unfinished sentences and other confusions. Moreover, when we speak, we frequently use the tone of our voice, pauses and variations in the speed, as well as the words themselves, to convey the desired meaning, and we add facial expressions and gestures to make it even clearer. If the person we are speaking to does not understand, he or she can ask questions, or demand additional information. The written word has to stand entirely on its own, and you will therefore have to make sure that you write down exactly what you mean to say, and that your reader is left in no doubt about how you intend the words to be read. You may be able to achieve the effect you want by the careful choice of your vocabulary, by the use of punctuation, and, where really necessary, by employing suitable adverbs.

On the other hand, although you must be aware of the dangers, you will almost certainly find that by writing as you speak you will have achieved that most desirable quality of simplicity.

Simplicity

Generally speaking, simple, straightforward writing is always best. Say what you want to say in direct terms, as briefly as possible, and you will achieve a far stronger effect than if you try to impress by using an inflated vocabulary and convoluted sentences. As a rule, short words of Anglo-Saxon origin are preferable to the long words which derive from Latin – so *chew*, for instance, should be more readily used than *masticate*, or *have* or *own* than *possess*. Of course, there are always exceptions to rules of this sort, and a longer, more formal-sounding word may sometimes be the right one, or indeed the only one, which will express exactly what you want to say. But always beware, unless you really know what you are doing, of using an outlandish word – the kind which is beyond a normal person's vocabulary – because it not only puzzles the reader, but draws attention to itself and away from the meaning of the passage in which it occurs. Simplicity is indeed a goal worth striving for.

Clarity

Make sure that you say what you mean to say. Take care with the words you use, and avoid malapropisms. Never allow ambiguities. If you are writing about two women, and use the pronoun 'she', you need to be certain that the reader will know which of the two women you are referring to. In the same way, ask yourself what the reader will understand if you write a sentence beginning: His report on the new regulation, which was highly controversial ... Is it the report or the new regulation which is controversial? Make it clear by rewriting. A couple of possibilities are: *His report, which was highly controversial, on the new regulation ...*, or *His report on the highly controversial new regulation ...* Make sure too that you have not created an ambiguity by placing a phrase in the wrong place, as in that celebrated advertisement, *For sale: large dog, will eat anything, fond of children.*

Similes and Metaphors, Adjectives and Adverbs

Poor writing is frequently overloaded with adjectives, metaphors and similes, which the author has included in an effort to achieve a richness of style. Such devices can help to provide an interesting texture in your prose, but they will not do so simply by being there in large numbers, or by any 'fancy' quality of their own; the richness comes when the writer has chosen them imaginatively and has used them only when they add essentially and effectively to the meaning; the more sparingly they appear, the more illuminating and powerful they will be.

Much the same can be said about adverbs. Mention has been made of the difficulty of conveying to the reader meanings which would be made obvious in speech by the tone of voice, and if you find yourself using a great many adverbs in an attempt to get such meanings across, see whether you can eliminate any of them, either because little doubt exists in fact about your intentions, or because it is possible to reword the sentence to clarify it.

In general, the more you restrict yourself to nouns and verbs, the more effective your writing is likely to seem.

Choosing Strong Words

We may call words weak or strong according to the sharpness of the images which they produce in our minds. Strong words conjure up pictures which are clear and well-defined, while those produced by weak words are fuzzy and indistinct. Taking nouns, for instance, those which may be called 'concrete', because they describe physical objects, such as *animal, tree, woman*, are much stronger than those we call 'abstract', which deal with concepts and emotions, such as *beauty, friendliness, cupidity*. The concrete nouns create definite pictures, but it is difficult to be sure exactly what constitutes *beauty, friendliness* or *cupidity*, especially in visual terms. If we then look at nouns with even more specific meanings we see that, for instance, *lion, oak* and *Mary* are all much stronger than *animal, tree* and *woman*, precisely because they produce more clearly defined images.

The same comments apply to many adjectives, adverbs, verbs, and indeed almost any word you can think of. Choose strong words when you can.

Avoid circumlocutions and hints in favour of definite descriptions – for instance, see how much stronger it is to say *It made him laugh*, rather than *He was greatly amused by it*, because, once again, the image is clearer.

Try not to use the passive voice of verbs, which usually results in a much more laboured and even pompous sound. *Mary Smith was presented with the prize by the mayor* sounds much more awkward than *The mayor presented the prize to Mary Smith* (although it must be admitted that in the latter instance the focus is less clearly on Mary Smith, which may not be the author's intention).

Clichés

We can barely open our mouths to speak without using a series of clichés, or hackneyed words and phrases. They come from many sources, including direct quotations or allusions to quotations, and similes and metaphors. Almost invariably, the words were striking when they were first used in that way, producing strong and splendid images, but they have been worn out by over-use. Too often we say or write a phrase such as *blissful ignorance* automatically – the words come naturally without a moment's thought. Or we describe a busy scene as *a hive of industry*, without bothering to see in our mind's eye the busyness of bees. These clichés have become weak, and their use makes an author sound tired and uncaring. You don't have to avoid them totally, but just make sure that if you do use clichés they are there because you can find no better way of saying what you mean.

Variety

Variety, if you will forgive a cliché after what I have just been saying, is the spice of life. It is also the spice of writing, and while all the points so far made in this chapter are, I believe, valid, a balance needs to be struck. If everything you write is 'strong', then the constant strength will somehow turn into weakness. You must have contrast and variety.

Repetitions

Occasionally, repetitions of words or phrases can be extremely effective, but it is a device to be used with the utmost care. The unintentional repetition usually sticks out like a sore thumb (another cliché) and is just as irritating to the reader. You must beware, on the other hand, of using too many alternatives in order to avoid repetition, which can be equally distracting. Many writers find it particularly necessary to substitute a whole series of words and phrases in place of, for instance, *John said* or *he said*. John (or he) becomes in quick succession *the former, the thickset man, the owner of the Jaguar, the financier, the proud husband*, and so on; while to avoid repeating *said*, the author comes up not only with *replied, answered, shouted* and the like, but also indulges in *gritted, gloomed, came the swift rejoinder* and similar absurdities, when the repetition of *John said* or *he said* would have been quite satisfactory.

Rhythm

One of the best bits of advice that any writer can be given is to read his or her work aloud, or, better still, have it read aloud to him or her, because the ear is so much better than the eye at picking up infelicities of phrasing, ambiguities and the like, and, especially, faulty rhythms. Any group of words has a rhythm, and it is something to which you must pay considerable attention if you want to improve your style. Beginners frequently produce a sequence of short sentences with the same construction, and therefore with jarring repetitive rhythms. Read the following passage aloud, and you will see what I mean:

> The man walked down the street, which was totally deserted. He paused by the jeweller's shop, glancing surreptitiously over his shoulder. The policeman stood on the opposite side of the road, and watched every movement. A sudden gust of wind swirled around the corner, snatching the man's hat away. It revealed the oddly dyed hair, so carefully concealed until then.

It would sound much better if rewritten to bring variety into the sentence lengths and their construction:

> The man walked down the totally deserted street, until he reached the jeweller's shop. There he glanced surreptitiously over his shoulder. The policemen stood on the opposite side of the street, watching every movement. A sudden gust of wind swirled round the corner, snatched off the man's hat and revealed the oddly dyed hair, which he had so carefully concealed until then.

Slang, Contractions, Dialect and Other Variations

Many would-be writers worry a great deal about the use of slang and of contractions such as *can't* or *wouldn't* or *I've*, feeling that informality is to be avoided at all costs. Well, yes, and again, no. It all depends on what effect you are trying to create, and on the sound or the rhythm of your sentences. In dialogue, informal contractions and slang are almost certainly not merely acceptable, but essential if you want to create a natural effect, though the usage will depend, at least to some extent, on the character of the person who is speaking. In straightforward narrative it is more usual to avoid slang and informality, but there is no rule against using them, and to do so occasionally may stop your work from sounding pompous. Let your ear be the judge.

Beware of using dialect or foreign words, or the jargon attached to a particular activity, such as a trade, unless you are sure that such words will be familiar to the average reader, or that their meaning is unmistakable from the context. To be presented with words which one does not understand is irritating, and the insertion of translations into the text, after the unfamiliar word, is as bad, if not worse.

Dialect can sometimes be validly presented in dialogue, but even then should be used sparingly. You can get as much effect from saying, *He spoke with a strong Cockney accent*, and then leaving your reader to supply the dropped aitches and strangulated vowels and glottal-stop t's, rather than splattering the text with apostrophes and attempting as Shaw did in *Pygmalion* to render the speech semi-phonetically – '*Wal, fewd dan y' de-ooty bawmz a mather should, eed now bettern to spawl a pore gel's flahrzn than ran awy athaht pyin.*'

Archaic words (*betimes, aught*, for example), vogue words (such as *parameters* or *yuppies*), poetic words (*ere* or *beauteous*) are best avoided unless they really belong to the period and the scene you are writing about, and even then best used with great discretion.

Tenses

Choose the appropriate tense for your writing. If you are producing a book similar to this one, you will probably use the present tense throughout, but although the present can be effectively used in fiction or biography or other forms, rather than the more usual past tense, you need to be a little wary of it, because in large doses it becomes rather obtrusive.

Do not mix the tenses in your narration. Stick to whichever tense you have chosen, at least for the main part, and if you change, for the sake of effect, keep the new tense going consistently and long enough for the reader to adjust to it and accept it. You might, for instance, wish to put an account of violent action in a thriller into the present tense for the sake of the immediacy it suggests, although the rest of the book is told in the past tense. But don't mix tenses within paragraphs.

The one exception to that rule is for flashbacks. Flashbacks often entail a great many pluperfect verbs – *He remembered the day he had first seen her. He had gone up to her, and had complimented her on her dress. She had smiled at him, and he had asked her to dine with him, and she had ...* Well, she had done this, and he had done that, and they had had a marvellous time, and all those 'hads' become very boring to read. It often works quite well in such cases simply to use the standard past imperfect: *He remembered the day he first saw her. He went up to her, and complimented her on her dress. She smiled at him, and he asked her to dine with him, and she ...* The introductory sentence in that example signals clearly enough that what follows is a flashback.

Grammatical Agreements

Try to make sure that everything you write is in agreement, in the grammatical sense. Verbs need to be singular or plural according to whether their subjects are singular or plural. The parts of speech in a list should be of the same kind – all nouns, or verbs, or adjectives. All sorts of words in a sentence need to agree with what has gone before – for instance, it is wrong to say *He played cricket, soccer, squash and swimming for his school*, because we do not 'play' swimming. It happens, by the way, to be a difficult sentence to get to sound right. If you say, *He played cricket, soccer and squash, and swam for his school*, it suggests that the only thing he did for the school was to swim. You could solve the problem by saying *For his school, he swam and played cricket, soccer and squash*, but the inversion (that is, putting *for his school* first in the sentence) makes it sound rather stilted, and you would probably have to end up by writing something much longer, such as *He played cricket, soccer and squash for his school, and also represented the school at swimming*. Perhaps a better solution would be *He was in the school teams for cricket, soccer, squash and swimming*. A problem such as that, incidentally, is a good example of the kind of difficulties which a writer often meets, the solution to which may take some time to find, and may involve several complete recastings of the sentence concerned before an acceptable version is found.

Keep Yourself Out of Your Writing

That may sound rather strange advice, especially since all writing must to some extent reflect its author. Obviously, you are in your work because the ideas and the words are yours, but, unless you are writing autobiographically, the reader should rarely be aware of you directly. This applies especially to fiction. You must not lecture your readers, and you must not explain to them things which are either obvious or better left for them to work out for themselves. You must not tell them that what follows is fascinating, or hilarious, or frightening, or anything like that – let them make up their own minds on such matters. Don't use exclamation marks (except perhaps in dialogue), because by doing so, you, the author, are saying to the reader, 'Isn't this funny ha-ha (or funny-peculiar, or whatever)?' If you are trying to write humorous material, don't be over-breezy, or lay on the irony too thickly – the best jokes are told in ordinary words which do not seek to be funny in themselves. The careful choice of words can be very important in creating atmosphere and effect, but the point is that the reader should never be aware that the author is trying to force the atmosphere and effect down his or her throat.

Revision

Unless you are a genius, your style will almost certainly be capable of improvement at the stage of revision. You should take endless pains over your revision – and it is something to be done not merely once, but as often as necessary to bring your work as near to perfection as you can. Look at every word you have written and ask yourself whether it is performing its intended and useful function, and whether it is the best possible word that you can put in that context. Check that you have written with clarity and simplicity, and with variety. Look out for and cut or alter unnecessary words, habit words (such as *of course, in fact, actually* – and I would add *you know*, if that boring, overworked phrase were not almost totally confined to the spoken word), repetitions (whether of individual words or of rhythms), and anything else which does not advance your story or your theme. Cut and cut and cut – the sparer your prose, the more sparkle it is likely to have.

Variations in Style

On the first page of this chapter I mentioned the need for flexibility in your style. The way you write must be influenced by the market for which you are aiming. While simplicity is always to be desired, however high the IQs of your potential readers may be and however complex your theme, there are degrees of simplicity. If writing a serious book for an adult market, or an article for such a paper as *The Times* you can use polysyllabic words and sentences with dependent clauses. On the other hand, if you are writing for small children, your style and vocabulary will probably be very basic (and far less demanding nowadays, incidentally, than those used by such writers as Beatrix Potter), and if your market is the tabloid press you will use short words, short sentences and short paragraphs.

Special Effects

The comments and suggestions made so far in this chapter are not rules, or if they are, they are rules which can be broken. If you know what you are doing, if you have an instinctive feeling for the use of words, you can break any number of rules. You can write a series of short staccato sentences or phrases without a verb in sight, or you can produce sentences of great complexity, which seem to go on for ever; you can write with a highly charged vocabulary or in dull and measured tones. If you have that special ability, your work can still be held up as an example of good and effective style.

Here is the first paragraph of *Judith*, a novel by that excellent Irish writer, Brian Cleeve:

> She stood listening. The wind battering at the house, the timbers creaking, cold whispers of air like the wind's spies, in the corridors, down chimneys, making the flame of her candle bend and darken, running the shadows on the kitchen floor, and cupboards. Her heart beating as she tried to listen, not to the huge buffets of the wind, the howling of it against roof and walls, the banging of loose shutters, the groaning of one of the great doors in the stable yard; not listening to any of those sounds, but trying to hear beyond them, under them, as if in such a gale she could hear their hoofbeats, men's footsteps, whispering.

It is basically a quite simple passage, but you could hardly say that the style is unobtrusive. Many of the sentences do not have proper verbs, and seem to be made up of lists. The whole paragraph is breathless, and possibly confusing, and yet the words have a very clear sense of having been chosen to present a series of the strongest possible images. The important thing is that it works. It is atmospheric and exciting, and it fulfils that essential purpose of an opening paragraph of making most readers want to know more.

Or take just half of the opening paragraph of *The Turn of the Screw* by Henry James:

> The story had held us, round the fire, sufficiently breathless, but except the obvious remark that it was gruesome, as, on Christmas eve in an old house, a strange tale should essentially be, I remember no comment till someone happened to say that it was the only case he had met in which such a visitation had fallen on a child. The case, I may mention, was that of an apparition in just such an old house as had gathered us for the occasion – an appearance of a dreadful kind, to a little boy sleeping in the room with his mother and waking her up in the terror of it; waking her not to dissipate his dread and soothe him to sleep again, but to encounter also, herself, before she had succeeded in doing so, the same sight that had shaken him.

It is hardly simple, with all those clauses and phrases enclosed in their pairs of commas; the language lacks excitement, and indeed has a certain heaviness; and the passage could be cut – oh, surely it could be cut! – to great effect. And yet to cut it would be to diminish its strength. Its structure is complex and its vocabulary is occasionally ponderous not merely because the novella was written nearly a hundred years ago, but because the author was intentionally creating an atmosphere of menace. Henry James is notorious for the convoluted quality of his prose, but he could also write extremely directly when he wanted to, and in this case the flat, deliberate approach is a preparation for the horror which is to follow, and a splendid example of an author not forcing his effects down his reader's throat by the use of emotive words.

In contrast to the two foregoing passages, here is a genuine extract from a letter received from a would-be author. The punctuation and spelling are both shown exactly as in the original.

> Notwithstanding after many Moons of tenacious struggle I finish what I consider to be a masterpiece,and yet not a single Publisher seems interested enough to as much as going beyond a brief synopsis,which does not reveal the unique novels true merits..A novel which I feel is abundant in literary merit-and with commercial possibilities -action, drama and

it's share of suspense,and what is more told in a true beleivability style.

Perhaps the author is a foreigner (which is the only reasonable explanation for such a strange jumble of words and the hopeless punctuation). The reader of this book may like to try his or her hand at amending the passage. In the meantime, I can only say that if the synopsis of the 'masterpiece' was all in that style, it is hardly surprising that no publisher was interested in reading more.

Some Do's and Don't's

AND/BUT
Teachers used to say that to begin a sentence with *and* or *but* was unacceptable, and to use either of those little words at the very beginning of a paragraph was considered even more deplorable. While there is no reason at all why you should not defy the teachers in this respect, you should be aware that you are placing an extra emphasis on the *and* or the *but*, and probably also on the sentence or paragraph which follows, if you do so.

AT THIS POINT IN TIME/IN THIS DAY AND AGE
Please, please say or write 'now' instead of these ugly, tautological clichés.

DIFFERENT
For many years it has been argued that you must use 'from' after 'different', rather than 'to'. The justification for 'from' rests on the fact that we say that something 'differs *from*' something, but recent editions of Fowler's *Modern English Usage* say firmly that 'different *to*' is justifiable. In any case, 'to' is so frequently used that many of us who still automatically say or write 'different *from*', do so more out of habit than because we believe it is the only correct form. What about 'different *than*', widely used in American English? 'From' or 'to' is usually to be preferred, but 'than' is neater in a construction such as *It is different than I thought it was*, when otherwise we would have to say, *It is different from (or to) what I thought it was*, or ... *the way I thought it was*.

DOUBT
You do not need to add 'but' when you use 'doubt' as a verb. For example: *I do not doubt that he will come*, not *I do not doubt but that he will come*.

EACH AND EVERY ONE

This is another popular expression which contains unnecessary words. 'Each' is quite capable of conveying the meaning on its own, and so is 'every one'. You don't need both.

'FOUR-LETTER' WORDS

In a period when freedom of expression is widely accepted, there is no reason why you should not use the so-called four-letter words if you wish. It is worth remembering, however, that they still retain some shock value, and if you want to use them in that way, then it works only if they are used sparingly. In other words, one four-letter word can be shocking; many four-letter words are usually boring. You should also bear in mind the audience at whom your work is aimed – don't expect to sell a story larded with the more offensive swear-words to the typical women's magazine.

HE OR SHE

An author writing in general terms in the past could use 'he' and 'him', and the other masculine pronouns to cover both sexes. Feminism, with some justification, objected, and it is now necessary to say 'he or she' (and I suppose one should really vary it occasionally and put 'she or he'), 'him or her', and so on. It is a great pity that there is no easy way round this, for the 'he or she' construction is undeniably clumsy. One solution is to use plurals: if you say 'readers', for example, instead of 'the reader', you can then put something like *what readers want is something that they can understand,* rather than the awkward *something that he or she can understand* which would have to follow 'the reader'. However, to use the plural is not always the perfect answer.

Feminism has also been responsible for turning 'chairman' into 'chairperson' (which to many people has a faintly absurd sound) or 'chair' (which some find difficult to understand as anything but an inanimate object). Oh, dear. At least I do not find 'chairperson' and 'chair' quite so distressing as the 'ploughperson's lunch' which I have seen on some pub menus.

HELP

The use of 'but' in such a sentence as *I could not help but see what happened* is to be avoided. *I could not help seeing what happened* is simpler and better.

IF AND WHEN

Yet another example of unnecessary words. One or other will always do the job for you.

LITERALLY

The trouble with 'literally' is that we use it as an emphasis word, without stopping to think what we are saying. *It was literally raining cats and dogs*, we might say. Well, I doubt it. 'Literally' means that we should take what follows as being factually true, when we would normally look upon 'raining cats and dogs' as the sort of colourful and well-known idiom which is not to be taken at face value. If you write, *It was raining cats and dogs*, we know that it was really bucketing down; but if you say, *It was literally raining cats and dogs*, then you can only mean that cats and dogs were actually falling out of the sky, like rain. It is probably best to avoid using 'literally' as much as you can, and if you do use it, make sure that you mean it – literally.

This is perhaps an appropriate place to mention words like 'terribly' and 'awfully', which we also use, at least in speech, as emphasis words. If you say, *It is terribly cold today*, we know that you don't really mean that it is so cold as to terrify us, and if you tell us, *It's awfully funny*, you don't expect us to believe that you have been overcome by awe at the humour of whatever it was. By all means include such usages in dialogue if it seems natural to do so, but you should be aware that you are debasing the words if you use them elsewhere simply as an emphatic substitute for 'very' or 'extremely'.

NICE

Many people were taught as young children to avoid the word 'nice', meaning 'pleasant, agreeable', because, they were told, it is an over-used word, and weak into the bargain. Both accusations are valid, but there are many times when it is a useful word, and its very weakness can be a strength. It also has a number of other definitions, most of which are archaic, but it can still be used validly to mean 'precise', as in *a nice distinction*.

NONE

'None' is a singular word, a contraction of 'no one', in fact. Since it is so often followed by a plural – *none of them, none of the players* – there is a temptation to use a plural verb. The temptation should be resisted. For example: *None of them wants to come. None of the players is over twenty-five*. It has to be admitted, however, that many people will regard my insistence on a singular verb after 'none' as yet another piece of pedantic advice to be found in this book. The trouble is, of course, that one man's precision is another man's pedantry.

ONE
If you use 'one' as a pronoun (an indefinite pronoun), as in *One is aware of what is going on*, you must be careful not to follow it with a personal pronoun in any of their versions. So you must not say, *One is aware of himself*, but *One is aware of oneself*. (See also *They* below.)

ONLY
The pedantic insist that 'only' must be placed next to the word that it qualifies. *I only like milk chocolate*, they say, probably means that you like it, but you don't love it (because the 'only' is attached to the 'like'), and that if the sentence is to be given the meaning which the speaker probably intended, it has to be rearranged to *I like only milk chocolate* or *I like milk chocolate only*. The only thing you need to worry about is whether the sense is clear. In most cases it will be, because we are so used in ordinary speech to putting 'only' where it sounds right rather than where, perhaps, it ought to be. Just be careful with a sentence like *I only laughed*. Does that mean that you didn't do anything more than laugh, or that you were the only person to laugh? Probably the former, but it could mean the latter, and if that was your intention, you really ought to rephrase it to avoid any ambiguity.

PERSONALLY
'Personally' is often used unnecessarily in such sentences as *Personally, I am against it*. It may be argued that if the order of the words is changed to *I, personally, am against it*, an additional emphasis is added, but this is legitimate only if you are, for instance, contrasting a personal view with an official one, as in *I, personally, am against it, but in my capacity as a delegate to this meeting I have to vote in accordance with my members' views, and so have to say that I am in favour.*

PREPOSITIONS AT THE ENDS OF SENTENCES
There used to be a rule that prepositions should not be used at the end of sentences or clauses, but Winston Churchill pointed out the absurdity of rigid adherence to that convention in his ironic example, *up with which I will not put*. However, his mockery was a little unfair, since *to put up with* is a rather special case; like *jump at*, *stand for* and *face up to*, for example, it is a phrasal verb, and to separate the preposition from the verb sounds quite ridiculous, especially when, as in 'up with', two prepositions are involved. When a phrasal verb is not concerned, it may be better to avoid

placing the preposition at the end of a sentence or clause. *It was her sister to whom he was particularly attracted* is probably preferable to *It was her sister he was particularly attracted to* and *The cupboard, in which he had stored the food, was bare* is smoother in sound than *The cupboard he had stored the food in was bare.* In dialogue the rule should be to use whatever construction sounds most natural for the character concerned.

SPLIT INFINITIVES

Grammarians have been teaching for years that it is wrong to split an infinitive verb ('to' and the verb itself, as in 'to make', 'to run', 'to sing') by the insertion of an adverb, and have shuddered, for instance. at the phrase used in the introduction to the television series "Star Trek", *to boldly go where no man has gone*, which they would prefer to hear as *to go boldly where no man has gone.* By convention, infinitives should never be split, but it has to be admitted that there are occasions when adherence to the rule results in a clumsiness or an ambiguity which could be avoided by breaking it. Fowler's *Modern English Usage* gives two examples which it says (even if a little doubtfully) are acceptable: *to further cement trade relations* (if you say *to cement further trade relations* it is unclear whether the word 'further' belongs to 'cement' or to 'trade relations'), and *to better equip successful candidates for careers in India* (in which 'better' cannot easily be moved to another position without making the phrase sound awkward). In most cases, however, the rule is still valid, and you should try not to split your infinitives, even though you may be right to believe that common usage will eventually force us 'to readily accept' the practice.

THEY

'They' should not be used after words like 'each', 'anyone', 'everybody', which may sound as though they are plurals, but are, in effect, singulars. So you should not say, *Everyone knows that they must obey the rules*, but *Everyone knows that he or she must obey the rules.* The 'he or she' in that sentence sounds very clumsy, and although William Strunk, jun. and E.B. White in their excellent book *The Elements of Style* advise you to use 'he' in all such cases, that will not please the feminists. The only answer is to avoid the construction if you can (*Everyone knows that the rules must be obeyed*), or to argue that common usage makes 'they' acceptable.

UNIQUE

'Unique' is what is known as an 'absolute' word. It means 'the only one of its kind,' and therefore cannot be qualified. If you say that something is 'more unique' than something else, you are saying that both are unique, although their degree may differ; but that is nonsense. 'Almost unique' is acceptable, but 'very unique' and 'most unique' are not. 'Quite unique' is equally liable to condemnation, although it can be argued that in this case 'quite' is an emphasizer (like 'indeed'), rather than a qualifier. Like 'unique', 'perfect' is also an absolute word, and should never be qualified.

5   The Right Words

English is a hybrid language. It has grown principally out of Anglo-Saxon, Latin and Norman French, giving it roots in both the Germanic and Romance languages, and it has also adopted many words of Celtic origin, together with others from a number of different sources, including Greece, many parts of the Commonwealth and, more recently, the United States. There has never been, as in France, any attempt to keep the language 'pure', and the result has been a richness which no other language can equal. We have a wide vocabulary, with a large number of alternatives at our disposal for almost any idea we wish to express.

Moreover, except for 's to indicate possession and, more often than not, s for plurals, we have done away with the majority of inflexions (the endings to words which show whether they are nominative, accusative, genitive or dative, singular or plural), we have adopted a singularly simple form of grammar, and we allow ourselves the flexibility of using nouns as verbs and verbs as nouns. Despite its unparalleled virtues, English also has its drawbacks – it has quite extraordinary pronunciations which often bear no relation to the spelling, and almost all the rules we have, for such matters as the formation of plurals, the declension of verbs, and, indeed, spelling, are full of exceptions. All in all, English is a complex language.

It is also, of course, a living language – or, as a friend of mine prefers to call it, a 'growing' language – and is subject to change. This means not only that we adopt new words to fit modern technology, but that old words change their meanings or become confused with each other. These alterations often have to be accepted. We may regret that we can rarely if ever use 'gay' nowadays to mean 'light-hearted' or 'merry', since it has become a common term for 'homosexual', but there is nothing that can be done about it – the English language has 'grown' to accept the new meaning.

The richness, the complexity and changing usages place a burden on the writer to choose words as carefully and accurately as possible. Growth can be accepted, and indeed welcomed, but not when it leads to a weakening rather than a strengthening of the language. There are many words which are losing their precision or are simply wrongly used, often through confusion with a similar-sounding word. We can and should do something about this – a loss of precision in a language is always to be regretted, and while it may be funny to give words their wrong meanings when Mrs Malaprop says them, for writers it is a sin.

If you are at all uncertain of the meaning of a word, look it up in a dictionary (or check it in the list below). You may also find it surprisingly useful to see what Fowler's *Modern English Usage* has to say. 'Fowler', as amended by Sir Ernest Gowers, is a fascinating book; it will not only offer guidance on such matters as split infinitives and which preposition should follow the word 'different', but if you look up 'jocose', for example, it will distinguish between a host of words with very similar meanings – 'arch', 'facetious', 'flippant', 'jesting', 'jocose', 'jocular', 'merry' and 'waggish'; it is also an amusing book – see, for instance, what it says about the pronunciation of 'margarine'.

Some of the Most Frequently Confused or Misused Pairs of Words

A/AN
Do you use 'a' or 'an' before a word beginning with h? Although *an hotel* is frequently seen, in fact the only words beginning with h where 'an' is needed are those in which the h is silent, such as 'heir' and 'hour'.

ACCEPT/EXCEPT
I would not have expected confusion between these two words – to 'accept' is to 'receive' or 'agree to', and 'except', as a verb, means 'leave out'. However, I recently saw a form for a local club which said, *When excepted for membership, your subscription will become due*, and I don't think they really meant that.

ACUTE/CHRONIC
When these two words are used in connection with illness, 'acute' means 'sharp', or 'sudden', and often 'dangerous' – *He has acute appendicitis* – while 'chronic' refers to a lasting or continuing condition – *She suffers from chronic indigestion*.

AFFECT/EFFECT
'Affect' is a verb, and means, in its most common usage, 'to have an effect upon', or 'to alter' or 'to change' in some way. For example: *The closing of the road will affect many people.* Or, *He was badly affected by the disease.* 'Affect' also has other meanings, including 'to assume ostentatiously' (*He affects the manners of an aristocrat*), but these uses are less likely to be confused with 'effect'. 'Affect' can also be a noun, referring to a mental state, but this is a comparatively rare medical usage. 'Effect' is usually a noun, meaning 'result', but can also be used as a verb, when it means 'to carry out'. For example: *The effect of the road closure will be disastrous. The closure of the road will be effected on Monday.*

ALLUDE/ELUDE
'Elude' means 'escape from (a pursuer)', whereas 'allude' means 'refer to indirectly' (see *Allusion* below).

ALLUSION/ILLUSION
'Allusion' is widely used to mean a direct reference to someone or something, but strictly speaking should be an indirect reference in which the person or object alluded to is not named. For example: *He said that Britain had similar troubles, and although he did not mention Northern Ireland, the allusion to the troubles there was clear.* 'Illusion' means something false or deceptive. For example: *The belief that all writers can spell correctly is an illusion.*

ALTERNATELY/ALTERNATIVELY
'Alternately' means 'in turn' or 'one after the other'. For example: *He hit him with his right and left hands alternately.* 'Alternatively' suggests a choice. For example: *You can go to London by private car; alternatively, you can use public transport.*

AMEND/EMEND
Both these words mean 'alter', but 'emend' is specifically concerned with the correction of errors.

ANTICIPATE/EXPECT
These two words can be used synonymously, but 'anticipate' has the additional meaning of 'act in advance', and may therefore be ambiguous. For example: *She anticipated the outcome* could mean that she expected it, or that she took some action before it was known.

ANXIOUS/EAGER

'Anxious' is widely used when 'eager' would be preferable. *I am anxious to see you*, we say, but really mean that we are eager to do so. 'Anxious' should only be used when you wish to imply anxiety (and one is usually anxious *about* something). You could perhaps say, *I am anxious to see my dentist*. Even that, however, would probably be better phrased as *I am eager to see my dentist, but anxious about what he will do to me*.

APPRAISE/APPRISE

'Appraise' means 'judge', whereas 'apprise' means 'notify' or 'make aware of'. It is therefore wrong to say, *She appraised me of the situation, which she had apprised*. Tell her to go away and appraise the situation, and then come back to apprise you of it.

AS/LIKE

There is a rule for deciding when you should use 'as' or 'as if' and when you should use 'like'; 'like', it says, is never followed by a verb, whereas 'as' or 'as if' must be. So it is correct to say, *Fiona writes like a professional*, but wrong to say, *Fiona writes like she had studied with a professional*. However, there are some occasions when common usage allows 'like' before a verb, especially if the 'like' comes after 'feel' or 'feeling' – *I feel like abandoning the attempt to clarify this problem*. To overcome the difficulty, try substituting 'as' or 'as if' for 'like'. If the sentence still makes the same sense, you should probably not be using 'like'. If in those two sentences above you substitute 'as' or 'as if', you will get: *Fiona writes as a professional*, and *Fiona writes as if she had studied with a professional*. In the first of these, the sense has been changed so that the sentence now means that Fiona is, in fact, a professional writer, and you will need to return to 'like' to preserve the idea that she is not a professional, but writes with a pro's ability. In the second sentence, on the other hand, the original meaning is retained, and you will probably be well advised to leave the substitution in place.

AURAL/ORAL

'Aural' is to do with the ear and hearing, and 'oral' with the mouth and, especially, speech.

BALMY/BARMY

Both these words can mean 'fragrant', as when describing the pleasant air of a warm evening, but it is preferable to use 'balmy' in that context. Equally, both can mean 'soft in the head', but, in that sense, 'barmy' is more usual.

BERTH/BIRTH
'Berth' means 'the place where a ship lies' or 'position' or 'sleeping-place'. 'Birth' is, of course, to do with being born.

BORN/BORNE
These are both past participles of the verb 'to bear'. 'Born' is used exclusively intransitively (i.e. does not take a direct object) in the case of birth – *I was born in March*. But when the verb is used transitively, the correct form is borne – *She has borne several children*. 'Borne' is also used in reference to putting up with something or carrying a burden.

BROACH/BROOCH
'Broach' means 'introduce', when first talking about a subject. 'Brooch' is an ornament worn on the dress.

BUSINESS/BUSYNESS
'Business' means 'occupation, work, a commercial concern', whereas 'busyness' is the act of being busy.

CALLOUS/CALLUS
A 'callus' is usually a patch of hardened skin. For example: *The constant digging had left calluses on his hands*. 'Callous' can also be used as an adjective to describe such patches, but is more often given the meaning of 'insensitive'. For example: *His attitude towards her suffering can only be described as callous*.

CAN/MAY
It is when they are used in questions that these two words are often confused, 'can' frequently taking the place of the correct 'may'. *Can I do something?* means *Am I able to do it?*, whereas *May I do something?* means *Am I allowed to do it?* Many readers will have discovered the difference while in school: *Can I leave the room, sir, please, sir?* And the teacher replied (at least, some of mine did), *You certainly can. The question is whether you may!*

CENSER/CENSOR/CENSURE
A 'censer' is the utensil in which incense is burnt, while a 'censor' is a noun meaning someone who inspects documents, films, etc. in a search for offensive material, or a verb indicating the removal of

such material. 'Censure' is similarly both a noun meaning 'blame, criticism', and a verb meaning 'to blame, to criticise'.

CHRONIC/ACUTE (see ACUTE)

COMMON/MUTUAL
These words both have to do with sharing. 'Mutual' is, strictly speaking, a sharing which refers to something which two (or more) people feel about each other. For example: *My wife and I have a deep mutual affection.* For anything else which two or more people share, but which is outside or apart from themselves, the proper adjective is 'common'. Therefore, *We share a common birthday.* The trouble, of course, is that 'common' has another, and unpleasant, meaning. That, presumably is why Charles Dickens called one of his novels *Our Mutual Friend*, when he really meant either *Our Common Friend* (which sounds as if the friend were vulgar) or *The Friend We Have in Common* (which is clumsy). In any case, *a mutual friend* is such a commonplace usage that we all know what is meant, even if it is not strictly correct.

COMPARED TO/COMPARED WITH
'Compared to' should be used in pointing out similarities between the things compared, and 'compared with' in pointing out their differences.

COMPLACENT/COMPLAISANT
These two words are very similar in meaning, and can both be used in the sense of 'obliging', but 'complacent' has the primary sense of 'self-satisfied', while 'complaisant' is often used, for instance, to describe a husband who does not object to his wife having a lover.

COMPLEMENT/COMPLIMENT
'Complement', as a noun, means something complete. For example: *The complement of a team in 'University Challenge' is four students.* As a verb, 'complement' means 'make complete or perfect'. For example: *The team was complemented by the addition of Joe Bloggs.* A 'compliment', on the other hand, is what someone pays you when they praise you. The word can also be used as a verb. For example: *He complimented her on her appearance.*

CONFIDANT/CONFIDENT
A 'confidant' (with a final e if female) is someone in whom someone else confides. 'Confident' is an adjective meaning 'sure'.

CONTINUAL/CONTINUOUS
These two words are so close in meaning as to be frequently confused. 'Continual' means 'very frequent', while 'continuous' means 'without a break'.

COUNCIL/COUNSEL
A 'council' is an assembly, as in *the town council.* 'Counsel', on the other hand is used as a noun to mean 'advice' or 'someone who advises', and as a verb to mean 'give advice to'.

CROCHET/CROTCHET
'Crochet' is a kind of needlework. A 'crotchet' is a hooked instrument or a short musical note, and from it we get the word 'crotchety'.

CROTCH/CRUTCH
All too often 'crutch' is used where 'crotch' is meant. A 'crotch' is a fork, and 'the crotch' usually means 'the fork of the body'. A 'crutch', on the other hand, is some kind of support, such as the implements that people use when they have damaged a leg. If you say, *He kicked him in the crutch,* it is unlikely to have hurt him very much, since the crutch was probably made of wood or metal. A kick in the crotch would be much more painful.

DEFINITE/DEFINITIVE
'Definite' means 'certain' or 'fixed'. It can also mean 'final', which is confusing, since the element which is always present in 'definitive' is finality – *a definitive book,* for instance, is one which covers its subject once and for all.

DEPENDANT/DEPENDENT
These words are interchangeable, but 'dependant' is usually used as a noun, referring to someone – a child, for instance – who is maintained by someone else, and 'dependent' is the favoured form for the adjective. You could say, for example: *His dependants are dependent on him.*

DEPRECATE/DEPRECIATE
The prime meaning of 'deprecate' is 'to pray against (something which is wrong or evil)', but it is more often used nowadays in the sense of 'disapprove of'. 'Depreciate' means 'to reduce or fall in value'.

DERISIVE/DERISORY
The difference between these two words is a subtle one. 'Derisive' is something which *shows* derision or mockery, whereas 'derisory' is applied to something which *deserves* derision or mockery.

DESERT/DESSERT
'Desert' is a noun meaning 'wasteland' or a verb meaning 'abandon'. 'Dessert' is fruit or a sweet served as the last course of a meal.

DISCREET/DISCRETE
The word which we usually want is 'discreet', meaning 'capable of keeping one's own counsel'. 'Discrete' is a comparative rarity, and means 'separate, distinct'.

DISINTERESTED/UNINTERESTED
'Disinterested' means 'impartial, without bias', while 'uninterested' means that the subject has no appeal to the person concerned. For example: *The referee for the League Cup is fair because he is a disinterested party; on the other hand, John does not care who wins, because he is uninterested in football.*

DUE TO/OWING TO
These two phrases are almost interchangeable. Use 'owing to' when you could equally well say 'because of', and 'due to' when you could replace it with 'as a result of'.

EAGER/ANXIOUS (see ANXIOUS)

EERIE/EYRIE
'Eerie' is an adjective which means 'strange and frightening', whereas 'eyrie' is the nest of a bird of prey.

EFFECT/AFFECT (see AFFECT)

ELUDE/ALLUDE (see ALLUDE)

EMEND/AMEND (see AMEND)

EMINENT/IMMINENT
'Eminent' means 'distinguished', while something which is 'imminent' is about to happen.

EXCEPT/ACCEPT (see ACCEPT)

EXCEPTIONABLE/EXCEPTIONAL
Something which is 'exceptionable' is something to which exception can be taken, something disliked. 'Exceptional' means 'out of the ordinary'.

EXPECT/ANTICIPATE (see ANTICIPATE)

FARTHER/FURTHER
'Farther' is the comparative form of 'far', and therefore refers to a matter of distance, whereas 'further' means 'additional'. It is wrong to say, for instance, *John went further than Mary* – he went farther than Mary – but correct to say, *John continued for a further three miles after Mary had stopped.* However, 'further' is nowadays so widely used when 'farther' would be more correct that only those who really care about the precision of the language will notice if you get it wrong.

FLAMMABLE/INFLAMMABLE
These two words mean exactly the same thing, 'capable of burning'. But because the 'in-' part of 'inflammable' sounds like a negative, 'flammable' is gaining some ground in manufacturers' warnings about the goods they produce, so that nobody shall be in doubt that something so labelled is not fire-resistant. 'Inflammable' is still, however, the preferred term in other contexts.

FLAUNT/FLOUT
'Flaunt' means 'display in an ostentatious way', but is sometimes mistakenly used nowadays where 'flout' is intended, with the meaning of 'disobey'. It is correct to say, *He flaunted his punk hairstyle,* but wrong to say, *He flaunted the law of the land* (when you mean that he disobeyed it). In any case, 'flout' is not simply a synonym for 'disobey'. It implies mockery, and means, when it is correctly used, 'act with contempt for', which is subtly, and importantly, different from 'disobey'.

FOREGO/FORGO
The verb 'forego' is used comparatively rarely, except in the forms 'foregoing' and 'foregone' – *the foregoing conditions* or *a foregone conclusion* – referring to something which has gone before, or has been said or written previously, or has been predetermined. 'Forgo' means 'do without'.

FOREWORD/FORWARD
'Foreword' is another term for an introduction or preface in a book. It is not spelt 'forward', which, whether used as an adverb, an adjective, a noun or a verb, has to do with being in front or in advance or going farther. You might think that a 'foreword', since it goes in the front of a book could be spelt 'forward'; it does, but it can't be.

FORMALLY/FORMERLY
'Formally' means 'in a formal manner', whereas 'formerly' refers to a former period, and can often be replaced by 'previously'.

GOURMAND/GOURMET
You will greatly offend a 'gourmet', who is a connoisseur of food and drink, if you call him a 'gourmand', for you will be saying that he is a glutton.

GRISLY/GRIZZLY
'Grisly' is an adjective for which we might substitute 'spine-chilling'. 'Grizzly' means 'grey-haired'.

HANGED/HUNG
'Hung' and 'hanged' are both past participles of the verb 'to hang'. 'Hung' is always used, except when you are referring to execution by hanging. So you say *The gold medal was hung around her neck*, or *The picture was hung in the Royal Academy*, but *The man was hanged*.

HOARD/HORDE
If you 'hoard' something, you collect it or store it, often secretly, or hide it, and what you have collected or stored is your 'hoard'. 'Horde' means 'crowd', and usually suggests that those who make up the crowd are unruly.

I/ME
The problem with 'I' and 'me' comes when they are used with other pronouns and linked by 'and'. People often say, *You and me will be there*, when the correct form should be, *You and I will be there*. And others, because they are aware that, in the first of those sentences, 'you and me' is wrong, then persist in saying or writing 'you and I' on every occasion, as in *He will talk to you and I tomorrow*. 'I' is the nominative case of a personal pronoun (and so are 'thou', 'he', 'she', 'we' and 'they'), and is used as the subject of a

sentence. 'Me' is in the accusative or the dative case (and so are 'thee', 'him', 'her', 'us' and 'them') and is used as the direct or indirect object of a sentence. ('You' and 'it' can be nominative, accusative or dative, so no confusion arises with their use.) Therefore, in these combinations, 'I' is used when the combination is the subject of the sentence, and 'me' when it is the direct or indirect object. For example: *He said that you and I should go*, but *He told you and me to go*, and *He gave the order to go to you and me*. You can usually tell whether you have got it right by dropping the 'you and' part of the sentence. You would not say, *He said that me should go*, nor *He told I to go*, nor *He gave the order to go to I*. You can use the same test if the pronouns concerned are any of those which have different forms in the nominative or the accusative.

Some people try to avoid the whole problem by using 'myself'. *My wife and myself are going to the theatre. You are coming to the theatre with my wife and myself.* Well, it's one way out, but you can tell just how silly it really is by dropping 'my wife' from those sentences. It would be much more natural to say, *You are coming to the theatre with me*, and you would surely never perpetrate such a line as *Myself is going to the theatre*. An additional difficulty comes in the answer to such a question as *Who's that? It's only me*, we reply, although we should, of course, say, *It's only I*. It has to be admitted, however, that in ordinary speech (and therefore in written dialogue) the correct form often sounds pedantic.

It has been suggested, incidentally, that the best way of getting 'I' and 'me' right is to follow the rule: use 'me' whenever you think you shouldn't, and use 'I' whenever you know you should.

Yet another difficulty arises with the question of whether you should use 'we' or 'us' in such phrases as 'we women' or 'we voters'. You would probably not say, *He told we voters to consider the matter carefully*, (it should be 'us voters', because in this case 'us' is the object in the sentence), but you might be tempted to say, wrongly, *Us women have got to stick together*.

ILLUSION/ALLUSION (see ALLUSION)

IMMINENT/EMINENT (see EMINENT)

IMPLY/INFER
'Imply' is much the same as 'suggest'. 'Infer' is similar to 'understand'. For example: *He implied that the situation would change. She inferred from what he said that the situation would change.*

INFLAMMABLE/FLAMMABLE (see FLAMMABLE)

INGENIOUS/INGENUOUS
'Ingenious' means 'clever' or 'imaginative', usually with the sense of the skill involved being unusual. For example: *He arrived at an ingenious solution to the problem* almost certainly means that he solved it in an unexpected way. 'Ingenuous' is much the same as 'naive'.

ITS/IT'S
Some time ago I was a judge for a short story competition. At one stage I considered the possibility of giving a prize to any competitor who knew the difference between 'its' and 'it's' – at least forty per cent of the entrants apparently didn't. 'Its' is the possessive version of 'it'. In other words, 'its' means something belonging to 'it', just as 'his' is the possessive version of 'he'. For example: *The outer skin of a tree is known as its bark.* 'It's', on the other hand, is simply a short way of saying 'it is', and the apostrophe stands (as it usually does) for a missing letter, which in this case is i. For example: *A tree has an outer skin; it's known as the bark.* Since 'it's' is usually something that we say, it is more likely to occur in dialogue than in other parts of your work, where you will probably use the full form, 'it is'.

LAY/LIE
The confusion between these two verbs is largely due to the fact that the past tense of 'lie' is 'lay'. It is therefore correct to say *I lay upon the bed*, provided that you are writing in the past tense, but wrong if you mean to use the present tense, when it should be *I lie upon the bed*. In the same way, *I'll go for a lay-down* is wrong; it should be 'a lie-down.' 'Lie' is an intransitive verb, whereas 'lay' is transitive and therefore always has an object. When you 'lay' something you are putting it down (or, if you are a hen, producing an egg, or, if it is a table, putting things down on it). So, if you insist on using 'lay' in the present tense when you are talking about reclining, you must say, for instance, *I lay myself down*. The past tense of 'lay' is 'laid'. For example: *I laid my arm on her shoulder.*

LEAD/LED
The problem here is that these two words can both be given the same pronunciation. 'Led' is the past tense of 'lead' (to rhyme with 'heed'), meaning 'conduct' or 'go before', but when 'lead' rhymes with 'head' it is the name of a metal. Therefore *She led me into the room* is correct.

LIBEL/SLANDER
Both these words are to do with something which destroys or severely damages someone's reputation. The principal difference between them is that 'libel' refers to the written word, while a 'slander' is spoken.

LICENCE/LICENSE
'Licence' is a noun, and 'license' a verb, so you might say, *The landlord has a licence to sell spirits. He is licensed to do so.*

LIE/LAY (see LAY)

LIGHTENING/LIGHTNING
'Lightening' is a reduction in weight. 'Lightning' is the electrical phenomenon which accompanies thunder.

LIKE/AS (see AS)

LOATH and LOATHE
'Loath' (which can also be spelt 'loth') means 'reluctant'. For example: *I am loath to punish you for so small an offence.* 'Loathe' is a verb meaning 'to hate, or find repugnant'.

LUXURIANT/LUXURIOUS
The word 'luxuriant' is used to describe something which is abundant and prolific. 'Luxurious', on the other hand, is usually used in the sense of 'with all the trappings of luxury, expensive and comfortable'. It can also mean 'lecherous', but this use is rare nowadays.

MANNEQUIN/MANIKIN
Both these words can mean 'model', but a 'mannequin' is alive and usually female and is employed to show off clothes. A 'manikin' is an artist's lay figure, or a figure used for demonstrations in medical schools, apart, of course, from its meaning of 'little man' or 'dwarf'.

MAY/CAN (see CAN)

ME/I (see I)

MENDACITY/MENDICITY
If you accuse someone of 'mendacity' you are saying that he is a liar. 'Mendicity', on the other hand, is the state or the act of being a beggar.

MILITATE/MITIGATE

As well as meaning 'serving as a soldier' or 'taking part in warfare', which are not the more common definitions of the word, 'militate' means 'conflict with' or 'be directed against', and is, indeed, usually followed by 'with' or 'against'. For example: *The actions of highjackers militate against one's confidence in the safety of air travel.* 'Mitigate', on the other hand, means 'make milder' or 'appease'. For example: *Her distress was mitigated by the fact that others were similarly affected.*

MUTUAL/COMMON (see COMMON)

NAUGHT/NOUGHT

Both words mean 'nothing'. 'Naught' usually appears in somewhat archaic sounding sentences such as *Naught availed him.* 'Nought' is the spelling we usually prefer when we mean the figure zero.

OF/'VE

One sometimes comes across 'of' wrongly used in dialogue in such a sentence as *I said I would of gone,* or *He'd of seen it if he'd looked properly.* What has happened is that the author has listened to the words in his head, but has not heard them accurately. He should have written *I said I would've gone,* or *He'd've seen it if he'd looked properly.* The confusion exists because in ordinary speech we often pronounce 'of' with exactly the same vowel sound (like the u in 'hut') as we use for ''ve'.

ORAL/AURAL (see AURAL)

ORALLY/VERBALLY

He said it verbally, we say. Of course he did – in that sentence 'verbally' is not needed. But what if we say, *He expressed it verbally?* All we are in fact saying is that he used words. 'Verbal' refers to words, whether they are in speech or writing. If you want to make it clear that the statement was spoken rather than written, you need to say, *He expressed it orally.* All contracts are 'verbal' – those which are not written down are 'oral contracts'.

OWING TO/DUE TO (see DUE TO)

PALATE/PALETTE/PALLET

The 'palate' is part of the mouth, and can also be used to describe a gourmet's sense of taste. A 'palette' is used by an artist to mix his colours. A 'pallet' is a straw bed or a wooden stand on which goods are stacked.

PASSED/PAST

It is perhaps not surprising that there should be some confusion between these two words when you consider the similarity in such sentences as *She passed by my window*, or *She had passed by my window*, and *She went past my window*. 'Passed' is the past tense or past participle of the verb 'to pass', and means 'went by' or 'gone by' in the sense of movement, or signifies a successful result in a test. 'Past', on the other hand, can be a noun or an adjective, referring to a previous time or period, or an adverb, meaning 'beyond' or 'from one side to the other'.

PIDGIN/PIGEON

'Pidgin' is the usual spelling for the special variety of broken English spoken in the Orient and the Pacific. 'Pigeon' is a bird.

PORE/POUR

I recently read a typescript in which the author had written at one point, *He was pouring over his book*. I wondered what he was pouring. Was it so hot that he himself had melted? Or was he pouring water over the book to quench its inflammatory ideas? Of course, the writer meant to say, *He was poring over his book*. 'Pore', as a verb, means 'study' or 'look at with close attention', while 'pour' is something which is done by or to liquids or by or to a stream of solids falling from one place to another or by people coming out in large numbers from, for instance, a theatre.

PRACTICABLE/PRACTICAL

'Practicable' means that the word it describes is capable of being put into practice. 'Practical' usually means 'sensible, helpful'.

PRACTICE/PRACTISE

'Practice' is a noun, and 'practise' is a verb. So, *The doctor practises medicine; his practice is in Birmingham*. Or, *It was her practice to practise the piano every day*.

PRINCIPAL/PRINCIPLE

One of the ways of distinguishing between these two words is to remember that 'principal' is the one which contains an a for 'adjective'. It is a rather solemn and impressive way of saying 'chief' or 'main'. 'Ah, yes,' you may say, 'but principal' is also a noun – as in 'the principal of a college'.' Well, up to a point, Lord Copper. It is really still an adjective, because in such a case it is an abbreviation for 'principal teacher' (or some such term). 'Principle', on the other hand, means 'origin' or 'fundamental truth' or 'moral belief'.

PRISE/PRIZE
'Prise' is the spelling usually used when referring to leverage. For example: *He prised up the lid of the chest.* 'Prize' is, of course, a reward, or booty, or can be used as a verb to mean 'value'. For example: *His most prized possession was the cup he won as the prize in the tournament.*

PROPHECY/PROPHESY
'Prophecy' is the noun, and 'prophesy' the verb. Most people get the latter right, but some try to spell the noun with an s.

RAISE/RAZE
'Raise' means 'lift up'. It is often wrongly used, by the way, in such a sentence as *He gave her a raise in salary* – it should be *a rise in salary*. 'Raze' means 'demolish'.

RESPECTFULLY/RESPECTIVELY
It is not surprising that these two words are sometimes confused, since they can both mean 'in a respectful, or careful manner', but 'respectively' is rarely used in this sense nowadays. More often, it has the sense of 'separately' or 'one by one'. For example: you could say, *He treated her respectively*, but you would be more likely to use 'respectfully' in that sentence. On the other hand, you would be wrong to use 'respectfully' in a sentence like *Messrs Smith, Jones and Brown are respectively Chairman, Secretary and Treasurer of the Club.*

RETCH/WRETCH
'Retch' (which can be pronounced either to rhyme with 'fetch' or to rhyme with 'each') is what you do when you are about to be sick, or feel like vomiting. A 'wretch' is an unhappy or unfortunate person.

SENSUAL/SENSUOUS
Both these words are adjectives concerning the senses, but 'sensual' is usually used with reference to sexual activities. So you might refer to *the sensual delight of copulation*, but to *the sensuous delight of swimming in a warm sea.*

SCEPTIC/SEPTIC
'Sceptic' (always pronounced as if it were spelt 'skeptic', as indeed it is in America) is a noun meaning 'someone who is unbelieving, or doubtful about something'. For example: *He is a sceptic when it comes to religion.* 'Septic' is an adjective referring to putrefaction. For example: *I have a septic toe.*

SHALL/WILL
There is a rule about these two words: if you simply want to express something in the future tense, you use 'shall' with 'I' and 'we', and 'will' in all other cases. For example: *I shall be there. The Government will take action.* But a determination to do something is expressed by using 'will' with 'I' and 'we', and 'shall' in all other cases – *We will make sure of it. You shall do as I say.* However, as these examples prove, the meanings can easily be confused, and the distinction between them is increasingly blurred. Much the same applies to 'should' and 'would', but of course 'would' also has the meaning of 'was in the habit of'.

SLANDER/LIBEL (see LIBEL)

STATIONARY/STATIONERY
Something which is capable of moving, but is not doing so, is 'stationary'. 'Stationery', on the other hand, is paper, ink, pens, paperclips, and all the other things that you would buy at a stationer's shop.

STRAIGHT/STRAIT
'Straight' means 'without bends' or 'honest' or 'direct'. 'Strait' means 'narrow' (hence 'straits', the geographical term referring to a narrow stretch of water). Apart from 'straits', it is normally used only in such combination words as 'strait-jacket' and 'strait-minded'.

THEIR/THERE/THEY'RE
'Their' is the possessive adjective pertaining to the pronoun 'they'. 'There' is an adverb of place. 'They're' is short for 'they are'.

TORTUROUS/TORTUOUS
'Tortuous' means 'winding, twisted', whereas 'torturous' is more closely allied to 'torture', and should refer to something painful.

TURBID/TURGID
People often talk about *turgid prose*, when they mean that what they have been reading is full of long words and complex sentences, and is generally hard to follow. The word they should probably be using is 'turbid'. 'Turgid' means 'swollen', and in respect of the written word is used to describe grandiloquent or bombastic work.

UNINTERESTED/DISINTERESTED (see DISINTERESTED)

'VE/OF (see OF)

VENAL/VENIAL
'Venal' means 'capable of being bought' in the sense of being bribed. For example: *He is thoroughly venal – he will abandon every principle if you pay him enough.* 'Venial', a word which is often applied to sins, means 'pardonable' or 'of minor importance as a fault'.

VERBAL/ORAL (see ORAL)

WAIVE/WAVE
In its commonest usage 'waive' means 'to give up a right'. The noun derived from it is 'waiver', used to indicate a statement relinquishing a right. 'Wave', as a verb, means a movement to and fro or up and down, and the noun indicates the shape which results from waving in the sea or the hair or in material, or the action of waving with the hand. 'Waver' can either mean 'hesitate', if it is a verb, or 'someone who waves', if it is a noun.

WHO/WHOM
'Who' should be used when it is the subject of a sentence. For example: *Who is going to be the next Prime Minister?* 'Whom' is used when it follows a preposition, or is the object in the sentence. For example: *To whom it may concern. It will be the person whom the Queen appoints.* ('Whom', in the second case, is the object of the verb 'appoints'.) Confusion arises when it is not entirely clear which word in the sentence is governing the 'who' or 'whom'. For example, it is easy to be misled into writing, *The Prime Minister, whom it is said is an autocrat, denied the charge.* In that sentence the pronoun is not the object of 'it is said', but of the second 'is', and the correct version would be: *The Prime Minister, who it is said is an autocrat, denied the charge.* On the other hand, it would also be correct to say, *The Prime Minister, whom his opponents have*

charged with being an autocrat, denied the allegation. In that case, 'whom' is the object of 'charged'.

WHO'S/WHOSE

These two are very like 'it's' and 'its'. 'Who's' is a contraction of 'who is' or 'who has'. For example: *Who's the man who's got the ball?* 'Whose' is the possessive version of 'who' or 'which', and therefore means 'of whom' or 'of which'. For example: *The man into whose hands the ball has fallen. The rose whose scent perfumed the room.*

WILL/SHALL (see SHALL)

WRETCH/RETCH (see RETCH)

YOUR/YOU'RE

'Your' is the possessive adjective pertaining to 'you'. 'You're' is short for 'You are'.

Single Problem Words

The following list includes some of the single words and usages which often cause difficulty, or the use of which is regrettable:

COMPRISE

This word means something like 'contain' or 'include' or 'be made up of'. So *A university comprises many faculties, but the faculties do not comprise the university.*

CRESCENDO

This is a musical term, indicating that the music should be played with gradually increasing volume. It is widely, and often wrongly, used in other contexts. If you say, *Her performance was greeted by a crescendo of applause*, you probably do not intend to say that the applause got louder and louder. Equally, you might write, *The crescendo of his career came with this appointment*, when you really mean 'the pinnacle' or 'the highspot'.

DILEMMA

A 'dilemma' is not any old problem, but means a situation in which there is more than one solution to a difficulty, neither or none of which is possible or will produce the desired result.

ENORMITY

'Enormity', though clearly connected with 'enormous', should always have the sense of wrongdoing rather than of mere largeness. For example: *The enormity of the drug trade*, but not *The enormity of Windsor Park*.

FORTUITOUS

'Fortuitous' means something which happens by chance, and is not a synonym for 'fortunate'.

GUESSTIMATE

This dreadful word has been formed on what I think of as the German habit of putting nouns together to make portmanteau words. (One of the most splendid, indeed, almost unbelievable, German examples is the 50-letter *Gesundheitswiederherstellungs-mittelzusammenmischer*, which means literally 'mixer-together-of-a-means-of-restoring-health', or, more simply and in a single word, 'dispenser'.) 'Motel' has been constructed on the same principle, but it is a useful word, combining elements of 'motor' and 'hotel' to produce a word for something which, when the name was first coined, was not easily and briefly described. 'Guesstimate', on the other hand, is a silly word, combining two elements which are already so similar that the new hybrid adds little to either. An estimate usually is a guess. I suppose that 'guesstimate' does suggest that the estimate is a very rough one, but my preference would always be, if a qualification is needed, for this to be effected by a suitable adjective ('careful', 'informed', 'rough', 'quick').

GRATUITOUS

'Gratuitous' can mean quite simply 'free', but is frequently used with the sense of 'uncalled-for, undeserved' (and therefore 'offensive'), as in *a gratuitous insult*.

HOPEFULLY

Those who care about language are, alas, fighting a losing battle over 'hopefully'. It should mean only 'in a manner full of hope'. For example: *She looked at him hopefully.* It is used nowadays so widely instead of 'It is hoped' or simply 'I hope', that such usage must soon become entirely accepted.

IRREGARDLESS

There is no such word as 'irregardless', although it is so often used nowadays, possibly because it seems to have an affinity with its synonym 'irrespective', that it may come to be accepted. It adds nothing in meaning to 'regardless' (which is simpler, and has two fewer letters if you are typing it).

LEADING QUESTION

A 'leading question' is not, as many believe, a particularly searching question, nor one which raises the most important point in a discussion. Most people know that the term comes to us from the legal profession, and that judges disapprove of it. In fact, it means a question which, by the way it is phrased, leads the witness towards the reply which the lawyer wants to hear. It might be difficult to answer if you were asked, *Who is the finest contemporary American novelist?*, but it is not a leading question. If, on the other hand, your inquisitor changed the wording, and said, *You would agree that Saul Bellow is one of the finest contemporary American novelists, wouldn't you?*, that is a leading question, because it was put in such a way as to show that the expected answer was 'Yes'.

NOISOME

This word has little, if anything, to do with noise. It means 'offensive' and is often used in connection with ill-smelling odours.

PRAGMATIC

'Pragmatic' can be used as a synonym for 'practical' or 'down-to-earth', but it is worth remembering that it also means 'officious' and 'opinionated', and overtones of those meanings may attach themselves to it.

PRISTINE

'Pristine' means 'pertaining to the earliest, or original, condition' of whatever you are talking about, or even simply 'ancient' or 'primitive'. So it does not necessarily mean 'clean and shining'.

TRANSPIRE

Do you feel at all uneasy when you use the word 'transpire' to mean 'happen' or 'come to pass'? Probably not, because it is commonly used in that sense. Purists will tell you, however, that strictly it means 'breathe through, or across', and that the only other sense in which it can properly be used is 'become known'.

6 The Right Length

Beginners often seem to be troubled by the questions of how long a sentence should be, of when to start a new paragraph or a new chapter, and of the desirable extent of a book. As with so many writing problems, there are no rules, and it all depends on what you are writing about, and on the market at which you are aiming.

Sentences

A sentence can be very short, consisting of one word only (although, technically, since it would have no subject, verb and predicate, it could not really be called a sentence), or very long, with a whole succession of dependent clauses. Normally, however, it consists of one thought or statement, expressed quite simply in a conventional form such as, for instance, *The old man sat in the chair by the fire*, or, a little more elaborately, qualified by additional clauses, as in *The old man sat in the chair by the fire, which was, as the regulars knew, reserved for his exclusive use because he had sat there every evening for the past twenty years.*

In general, it is wiser to avoid the extremes. One word 'sentences' can be very effective, but you need to be sure of your technique, and use them with discretion, so that the style does not become obtrusive. The kind of complex sentence which goes on for half a page can also work very well, but you need to be as good a writer as Henry James or Bernard Levin to get away with it, and you have to be sure that you are making sense to the reader and that he or she will not have forgotten by the end of the sentence what its beginning was. It is also important, as has already been pointed out earlier in this book, to have a variety in the length of your sentences, so that you avoid a monotony of style.

Make sure that your punctuation is adequate. Read the chapter on punctuation – especially the sections on the full stop and the comma – and follow the advice given there. It is worth repeating the suggestion that you should read your work aloud, slowly, listening carefully to the pauses that you make. Read the following sentence aloud: *If there is a longish pause, you have probably come to the end of a sentence, you need to break the piece there with a full stop.* Of the two commas in that sentence, the first, after *pause*, is adequate, but the second, after *sentence*, is not strong enough, and should be replaced by a full stop. Alternatively, you could use a conjunction: *If there is a longish pause, you have probably come to the end of a sentence, and can join the next sentence on by using a conjunction.*

Paragraphs

Like a sentence, a paragraph can consist of one word – *Silence*, for example, might easily stand on its own as a complete paragraph. More usually, the paragraph will be made up of a number of sentences, but they will be connected in that they will be concerned with one basic thought or group of thoughts. So if you move to a new point, or take a new subject, then you begin a new paragraph. Look at the three paragraphs under the heading Sentences above. Each contains a number of sentences connected by the basic subject of the paragraph: the first is a definition of a sentence, the second is about short and long sentences, and the third is concerned with the punctuation of a sentence.

Think of paragraphs, if you will, as Christmas parcels sent to various families. Within the parcel are individually wrapped presents – these are the sentences. The presents inside the parcel are all linked by being destined for one group of people, just as the sentences in the paragraph hang together because they are all concerned with the same theme.

As with sentences, it is advisable to avoid very long paragraphs, less because you are likely to confuse your reader than because a too solid chunk of type has a somewhat formidable appearance, and may be off-putting. It does depend to some extent, however, on the total length of the piece you are writing. If you are producing a full-length book you can afford to have fewer and longer paragraphs than if you are writing a short article. Even more influential in this matter is the audience for whom you are writing: if your work is intended for small children or for the tabloid press, your paragraphs will rarely contain more than two fairly simple sentences (indeed, in these cases you may need to break the work into very short paragraphs even if the sense does not demand it), while much longer paragraphs would be acceptable in a serious article or a book intended for a reader who will be prepared to give more concentrated and lengthy attention. Even then, however, and if only for cosmetic reasons, it may be wise to look at any paragraph which extends for a whole page or more and consider whether it can be broken at some point. It usually can be so broken. The paragraph we are in at the moment is not exceptionally long, but it is getting near the desirable limit, and if it were really necessary, could be broken after the words 'a short article' without destroying the sense, and without it being too obvious that a break was not originally intended at that point.

For dialogue, while it should be remembered that, once again, there are no inviolable rules, it is customary nowadays to start a new paragraph for each different speaker. The paragraph will, however, include not only the attribution (*he said, she replied*, etc.), but also actions or other material relevant to that speaker. For example:

> 'Are you going to the meeting?' Anne asked.
> 'Yes.' Malcolm walked over to the window. 'I'm not looking forward to it.' His voice was a mere whisper. 'Everything is bound to come out.'
> There was a brief silence, broken only by the sound of a distant aeroplane.
> 'I don't think I can face it,' he said at last.
> The anguish in his voice was so plain that she went to him. 'You must, my dear. But try not to worry about it.'
> He laughed bitterly.
> 'Oh, I know it's easy for me to say that,' Anne said, 'but please try.'

Note that there are new paragraphs to describe the silence, which is not part of Malcolm's speech or actions, and for his laughter, which interrupts Anne's speeches. There is also, despite the fact that Malcolm has just been speaking, a new paragraph beginning with a mention of the anguish in his voice, because the point of view has changed and we see the anguish through Anne's eyes. Never change the viewpoint within one paragraph.

If a speech in dialogue is particularly long, it may be worth breaking into two or more paragraphs, in which case you will open the quotation marks at the beginning of each paragraph, and not close them until the end of the speech.

Chapters

In his largely excellent book, *Writing a Novel*, the late John Braine perpetrated one piece of nonsense, when he advised that every novel should consist of at least twenty chapters. You can have as many or as few chapters as you like, depending on the style of book you are writing, and they can be very long or very short, and do not necessarily have to be of similar lengths. Especially if you are writing fiction and building up your narrative by means of a series of short scenes, you can even do without chapters altogether, but you will probably want to indicate breaks in the story by means of blank lines. On the other hand, for certain types of novel, especially of the kind which publishers call 'category fiction' (romances, westerns, crime stories), you may need to conform to conventions regarding both the number and length of chapters.

In non-fiction, each chapter will almost certainly deal with a different aspect of the subject, or perhaps, if it is a biography or history, with a certain period or group of events. The author of non-fiction will usually have little trouble in deciding when a new chapter is needed, although some problems may still exist, as for instance in this book, in which I have had some difficulty in making up my mind how to place certain material which could have found a home in a number of different chapters. This discussion of sentences, paragraphs and chapters could, for instance, have been part of the chapter on punctuation or that on style, but in the end seemed to me happier as a short chapter on its own. In the same way, new chapters in fiction may begin because of a change of scene or of time or because the author is going to focus on a different character. After all, we speak of someone beginning 'a new chapter in his life', and if you think of what you are writing in those terms, you will perhaps have less difficulty in deciding when a new chapter is required. Alternatively, think of commercial television's 'natural breaks'; because of the needs of the advertisers, not all breaks in the programmes are as natural as they might be, but whenever possible, the programme breaks at a point when a new scene or development or argument is about to take place.

Something else which can be learnt from television is that those who decide when the breaks shall come try to place them at a point where the interest of viewers has been not only sufficiently aroused for them to want to go on watching, but preferably has reached a point when they cannot bear not to know what happens next. In other words, the break comes immediately following a 'hook', a 'cliffhanger'. The need for a hook was something else which Mr

Braine stressed, and this time with much more sense. So end your chapter, if you can, when a crisis of some description has been reached, and your hero or heroine is facing a dilemma or a major change in circumstances.

Chapter titles are almost always needed for non-fiction, but are rarely seen nowadays in novels.

Book Lengths

A question with which all teachers of creative writing are familiar is how long a book should be. The obvious answer is that any book should be long enough to cover its subject adequately, whether it is fiction or non-fiction. It should never be padded, and indeed there are very few books, even those which are extremely successful, which would not benefit from cutting, since most authors tend to overwrite rather than underwrite. But the would-be writers are really asking what length of book is acceptable to publishers.

Excluding books for children, which are almost always shorter than the general run of books for adults, the range is enormous. If you are writing romantic fiction a length of between 45,000 and 55,000 words is more or less standard, and much the same applies to the average western or crime book that you may see on the library shelves (check requirements with the publisher to whom you intend sending your work); family sagas and some historical novels tend to be longer, simply because they cover a wider canvas. But there are no rules; very short books get into print, and so do enormous tomes of 1,000 pages or more. All that can usefully be said is that, generally speaking, publishers are unlikely to be enthusiastic about submissions from unknown authors which are less than 40,000 or more than 120,000 words, and the reason for this is largely one of publishing economics. The length is perhaps less critical for non-fiction, partly because a publisher has greater freedom in the pricing of such books (fiction tends to appear at standardized prices).

Unless you are aiming at the library fiction market, it seems wiser to me not to start out with a specific word length in mind, or, at least, without more than a rough idea of how long the book will be. Let it decide its own length. If, when you are part way through, it becomes clear that it is going to be an extremely short book, you may need to ask yourself whether your material is substantial enough to form a book, or whether it might be more suited to a series of articles or a short story; equally, if the book looks like turning into a 1,000 page whopper, perhaps it is worth checking to see whether you are overwriting or whether the work could be split up to make more than one volume. Don't worry about it too much – no publisher is really daunted by the length of a book if it is of exceptional quality.

PART TWO

Getting Into Print

Almost anyone can be an author; the business is to collect money and fame from this state of being.

A.A. Milne

7　Presentation of Your Work

Is the way you present your work to a publisher important? Yes, it is – very important. You are working in a crowded market, and every editor receives and considers hundreds of submissions every year. Many are not publishable, because the author is without talent, or even illiterate, or because the work is grossly libellous, or for many other possible reasons. But if you and your work do not come in any of these categories, however wonderful your writing may be, if it looks a mess you are putting a barrier in the way of its publication. A neat, legible typescript, well set out, stands a much better chance, not only because it is easier to read (being human, editors do like something which is easy on their eyes), but also because it suggests that you have a professional attitude. If the editor senses, even before starting to read, that you care enough about your work to have presented it well, you have already chalked up a bonus point.

However badly you present your script, provided it is typed (see below), the publisher will undoubtedly give it some consideration, just in case it turns out to be a masterpiece. (It really is a myth that publishers do not even glance at everything that any author may send in; some material may, however, be given little more than a glance if, for various reasons, such as total illiteracy, or being on a subject which that particular firm never publishes, the submission is obviously unsuitable.) But if your work is no more than averagely good and is sloppily prepared, it may soon be abandoned in favour of one of the neater typescripts among the pile on the editor's desk.

Of course, the finest presentation will not help if your work is not up to the standards required, or if you have submitted something which is unsuited to the publisher's needs, but you will never help yourself by poor presentation.

General Matters of Presentation

TYPE YOUR WORK

Although a few magazines will occasionally accept handwritten articles (provided that your handwriting is consistently legible), almost all publishers expect work to be typed, especially if it is at all lengthy, and most book publishers will refuse to consider handwritten submissions.

What can you do if you don't type? You can take your work to a typing agency or to one of the many people, usually ex-secretaries, who do such work at home (you will find them in the small ads section of your local newspaper or of any magazine for writers). You may think that no one would be able to read your writing and cope with your crossings-out and insertions and so on, but those who undertake this work are usually used to pretty messy handwritten material. They will often correct your spelling and punctuation, if you ask them to do so. You will naturally need to go through the work when it comes back to you to check it for any mistakes, but in most cases you will have an accurate typescript with a professional appearance. Unfortunately, this method is going to cost a fair amount.

An alternative is to buy a second-hand typewriter, take an evening class course in typing, or even teach yourself to type, which is not as difficult as you might think. You will be slow at first, but although you may never approach the speed of a trained touch-typist, you can soon become reasonably proficient, even if you only use two fingers. Your script should be typed in double spacing. Never use single spacing (except for poetry and plays – see below), even for footnotes. If you are including a long extract from some other book, which in the printed form will probably appear in a smaller size of type than the rest of the text, it may be a good idea to indent each line in your typescript to distinguish it from the rest, but it is still better in double spacing. Double spacing is far easier to read, and also allows room for occasional corrections or insertions. Some authors use one-and-a-half spacing, presumably in order to save paper, but the saving is just not worthwhile. Type on one side of the paper only. Apart from the fact that if you use both sides, the typing on one side may show through on the other, again a typescript is physically easier to read if only one side is used.

Try to use the same typewriter throughout. 'Well, of course,' you may say. 'I've only got one, anyway.' But some authors submit books which have apparently been typed on half a dozen different machines, with different sizes and styles of type. It doesn't look good, and it makes the job of estimating the length of the book much more difficult.

Do make sure that you use a new, or reasonably new, black typewriter ribbon. Writing is not a wildly expensive occupation as far as the materials are concerned, but many authors seem to begrudge spending money on typewriter ribbons, and submit work which is typed in a faint shade of grey. You can't really blame an editor who looks at such a typescript and decides that it's just not worth straining his or her eyes to read it. If you are writing a book, it is a good idea to start off with a new ribbon, and, if the typescript is more than about two hundred pages long, to replace the ribbon halfway through. The same applies to word processors (see below). Don't, by the way, buy a two-coloured ribbon (unless you want the second colour for some other purpose than preparing a typescript for a publisher) – it is preferable that your work should be in black throughout.

CARBONS

You will need to make copies of your work. If it is accepted for publication, the publisher will almost certainly ask for a second copy, and sometimes wants a total of three. Additionally, you must have a copy for yourself (in case your original gets lost, or to refer to if necessary). If you are using carbons, again please do not economize on them. Many authors are even meaner about carbon paper than about typewriter ribbons. As soon as your carbons begin to give a grey and fuzzy impression, discard them and use new ones. In general, publishers like to see the top copy rather than a carbon, principally because the top copy is usually easier to read, but also because they suspect, if you send a carbon, that you have submitted the top copy elsewhere – which they don't like, unless you have told them that you are doing so and they have agreed to consider the work on that basis (see the section on multiple submissions on page 123). However, a photostat is usually acceptable, provided of course that the original which you have copied was good enough to give a clean, legible stat.

PAPER

The most acceptable size of paper nowadays is A4 (210 x 297 mm). Quarto is still used, but other sizes, including foolscap and most certainly anything smaller than quarto, are not to be recommended. If you are submitting your work in the United States, it is best to use their equivalent of quarto, which is slightly larger than the British variety (11″ x 8″). Use a 70 or 80 gramme bond paper for your top copy; bank paper (the flimsy kind) is usually acceptable for copies.

LAYOUT

Always leave good margins. I would suggest that these should be a minimum of an inch at the top and on either side, and an inch to an inch and a half at the foot of the page. There are three reasons for this: firstly, yet again the typescript in this form is easier to read; secondly, the margins leave room for an occasional insertion and for the publisher's instructions to the printer; thirdly, when the printer sets the book up in type, he clamps the page he is transcribing in a stand, and if there are inadequate margins, the clips will obscure part of the text.

Do not leave a blank line between paragraphs, unless it is your intention that a blank line should appear in the printed version to indicate a change of scene or of subject – in which case it may be wise to place an asterisk in the centre of the otherwise blank line to make sure that what you mean is clear.

EMPHASIZING WORDS

If you want a word to appear in italics, underline it. If you have a particularly clever typewriter or a word processor, don't use its facility for typing in italics, which may not always be clear. Underlining is always understood by the printer to mean that italics should be used. On the whole, you should not use capital letters for emphasis, unless you have already used italics and now want to indicate something even stronger, as for instance, in such a line of dialogue as: 'She didn't,' he said. 'She *didn't!*' His voice rose to a shriek. 'She DIDN'T!'

WORD PROCESSORS

More and more authors are turning to word processors for their work, especially now that capable machines are available at a low cost. If you buy a word processor, be prepared to spend some time learning how it works – it may be a few weeks before it becomes 'transparent' to you, which is to say that you can make it do what you want without having to consult the manual every time (and, incidentally, the manuals are notorious for being difficult to understand). It is worth persevering, however, for you will find that the word processor has two enormous advantages: it makes corrections and major alterations to the text simple to carry out (and many writers find that this facility actually improves the quality of their work), and it takes the drudgery out of producing the final copy. It used to take me several weeks to type the final copy of a long novel, but with my word processor, I now print it in one or two days.

If your word processor has a daisy-wheel printer, you should have no problems with the appearance of your typescript as long as you don't use tired old ribbons. It will look like good, even typing. Dot-matrix printers, on the other hand, in which the letters are made up of tiny dots, produce work which is often less easy to read, especially if you have the kind which condenses the ascenders and descenders (the uprights on the letters b, d, h, etc., and the tails on the letters g, p, y, etc.). You may have the facility with a dot-matrix printer for using either draft or high quality printing, and you will probably want to choose the former. The high quality is obviously very much better, especially with punctuation, which is often very faint in the draft quality mode, but the problem is that high quality printing is so slow, and can take more than twice as long. If you use the draft quality, change the ribbon frequently so that you get as good an impression as you can. One possibility is to use high quality for the top copy and draft quality for the duplicates.

It may not be necessary for you to print your work at all if the publisher has word processors in the office, and the machines are compatible with yours. In such cases, you may be able simply to supply copies of your discs which the editor can then read on an office machine. However, you would need to check first whether the publisher would be willing to consider your work in this form. You should, of course, keep duplicates of the discs, and it is also advisable to have a print-out in case the discs should deteriorate, or part of the text should be wiped off by mistake.

CORRECTIONS
However desirable it may be, it is not absolutely necessary to present a perfect typescript. An occasional correction or insertion is permissible, provided that it is legible (unless your handwriting is always perfectly clear, it is better to use the kind of printing that small children learn, rather than 'joined-up' writing). Once a page starts looking messy, it is worth taking the trouble of re-typing it. If, after you have typed the whole of a long book, you have a lengthy insertion to make on, say, page 31, re-type the page to make pages 31 and 31a, and then add a note to say 'continue on page 32'.

MAKE SURE YOUR TYPESCRIPT LOOKS FRESH
If you have submitted the same work to several publishers, it is likely that the typescript will be looking rather battered. If you

cannot afford the time or the cost of re-typing the whole thing (so easy on a word processor, of course), at least re-type the first page and any others which have become crumpled or have acquired coffee stains.

COPYRIGHT

Anything which you write is your copyright (unless you assign it to someone else), and it is therefore not necessary to put a statement to that effect on your typescript. It will do no harm, however. Such a copyright notice should be in the form 'Copyright © John Smith 19——'. Strictly speaking, you should use your full name ('John Brian Smith', for example, rather than 'John Smith' or 'J.B. Smith'), and it should be your real name and not the version of it which you use as an author or a pseudonym. However, this rule appears to be rarely honoured, and it is possible to copyright the work in virtually any name you like to use. The date will of course be the year in which the piece was written, but the publisher will change it to the date of publication when the work appears in print.

Titles are not copyright, but you should avoid using one which is already very well known. If you were to call your novel *The Day of the Jackal*, for instance, you could be sued for 'passing off' (that is to say, for misleading potential purchasers into believing that the book was the famous thriller by Frederick Forsyth – see page 131).

Ideas for books are not copyright either, and many authors fear that if they put up a project to a publisher, he may reject their work but then pinch the idea and give it to another author. It is not common practice among reputable publishers to behave in this way, but it does occasionally happen. If you believe you have been victimized, it is perhaps worth considering the possibility of legal action, but it may be difficult to prove that the theft of your idea was deliberate, rather than merely coincidental.

PERMISSIONS

Of course, just as your own work is copyright, so is that of other writers, at least, in most cases, until fifty years after their death. If you wish to quote more than a few words from someone else's book, or to use illustrations which are not your property (photographs of people, incidentally, are the copyright of the photographer, not of the subject, unless some prior arrangement has been made to vary this rule), you will have to obtain permission, and often pay a fee, in order to do so. There is no need, however, to seek such permissions before you are certain that the work is going to be published. At that stage, your publisher will be able to give you advice on how to proceed.

Now for some more specific points depending on the nature of your work:

Books – Fiction and Non-Fiction

LAYOUT
You should try to keep the same number of lines on every page. If you use a word processor which has a facility of rejecting 'widows and orphans' (a single line separated from the rest of the paragraph either at the top or the bottom of a page by a page break), you should override the command. If you do not do so, the number of lines may vary from page to page. Widows and, to a lesser degree, orphans are to be avoided in printed work, but do not greatly matter in a typescript.

Begin chapters on a new page. There is no need to start them halfway down the page, but it looks better to leave two or three blank lines at the top, then to have the chapter title (or 'Chapter One' or '1', for example) and then another blank line before the text begins.

Indent your paragraphs – five spaces at the beginning of the line are adequate to avoid any confusion, while anything more than ten spaces is unnecessary.

Be consistent in all these matters.

OVERLAP WORDS
Some authors put the first word of the next page at the foot of the page on the right, sometimes in brackets. This may help the reader to be sure that the pages are in the right order, but it is not necessary to use overlaps, and some editors find it positively irritating.

PAGE NUMBERING
Always number your pages. It does not matter whether you put the number at the top or at the foot, in the middle or at the right-hand side. But please number the typescript consecutively from the beginning to the end – that is to say from 1 to 237 (or whatever is the last page). Do not start again at 1 with each chapter. If you wish, you can also put the title, or a shortened version of it, or your name beside the page number (e.g. 'NUTS.1, NUTS.2 etc.' or

'Legat.1, Legat.2 etc.'), but this, though helpful if your typescript should get mixed up with someone else's, is not strictly necessary.

PRELIMINARY PAGES
The 'prelims' are the pages in a book before the text begins. In a printed book they usually include: a half-title page (on which only the book's title appears), on the reverse of which may be placed a list of other books by the same author, or volumes in the same series; a title page (which gives the title, author's name and publisher's name)', and on its reverse an imprint page, sometimes called a biblio page (which gives the book's printing history, copyright notices and the printer's imprint). The prelims may also include a dedication, list of contents, list of illustrations, foreword, etc.

Your typescript does not need a half-title page or an imprint page. The publisher will prepare these if the book is accepted. He will also supply an ISBN. ISBN stands for International Standard Book Number. Each book, including different editions (but not straightforward reprints) of the book, has its own individual number, which also identifies its country of origin and its publisher. The publisher allocates ISBNs to the books when they are scheduled for publication.

The typescript should, however, have a title page, on which you should have typed (don't draw it in fancy lettering) the title, the author's name or pseudonym, and his or her name and address or agent's name and address. It is also helpful to show the approximate length of the typescript in the number of words. See example opposite.

Don't put 'First British Serial Rights' or 'F.B.S.R.' on the title page. That is something which goes on work submitted to magazines and newspapers, not on books sent to a book publisher (see page 111).

Whether you will have a list of previous books, a dedication, list of illustrations, a foreword, etc., depends on circumstances and your own wishes. Each should appear on a separate page in the typescript. If you have given titles to your chapters, or parts, you may wish to include a list of contents, but if you have simply called them 'Chapter 1, Chapter 2, etc.' it is probably not worth putting it in.

THE LAST PAGE
I would suggest that you should put your name and your address, or that of your agent, on the last page of the book. It is also quite a

THE NUTS AND BOLTS OF WRITING

Michael Legat

Approx. 60,000 words

Michael Legat
c/o Campbell Thomson & McLaughlin Ltd,
31 Newington Green,
London N16 9PU

good idea to put 'THE END' after the last words, especially if your book has the indeterminate kind of ending which is quite fashionable nowadays.

WORD COUNTS

You do not need to count every word in your book. Nor, if you have a word processor which counts the words for you, will the publisher wish to see the figure which it produces. The publisher wants a figure which takes account of short pages at the beginning and end of chapters, and of short lines. The way to calculate the wordage is therefore as follows:

Count the number of words in ten consecutive full lines on five different pages. You will then have counted fifty lines. Divide the total number of words in those fifty lines by fifty, to arrive at the average figure per line. If your total amounted to, say, 595, the average number of words per line would be 11·9. Next, count the number of lines on ten full pages; if you have been careful to keep the same number of lines on every page, you will obviously need to count one page only, but if the pages vary in length, then get to an average by dividing the total lines on the ten pages by ten. If your ten pages gave you a total of 275 lines, the average would be 27·5 lines per page. Now multiply the average number of words per line by the average number of lines per page. In the examples so far given the answer would be 327·25. Round the figure up or, in this case, down, and you get 327 words per page. Now multiply that figure by the number of pages in your typescript, ignoring the fact that some pages may be short. If, for example, your book has 219 pages, you would get a figure of 71,613. Round off the figure to the nearest thousand, and you would arrive at 72,000 as the wordage, and that is the figure which you would put on the front page.

This may sound very complicated, but it isn't really. If it totally baffles you, take heart – although many publishers like to see a word count, it is not absolutely essential to give one.

FASTENING THE TYPESCRIPT TOGETHER

There is considerable disagreement on this subject, although I believe most publishers are united in disliking the kind of typescript which is fastened together in one indissoluble lump – heavy to hold and clumsy to read. Even a ring binder can be awkward to work with. My own preference, in the days when I was a publisher, was always for separate sheets, held together only by being placed in the kind of box that typing paper comes in, or in a wallet-type folder, or by elastic bands round the whole thing. You could fasten your chapters or batches of pages together with paperclips or split pins, but I would not recommend either of these methods – paper clips have a nasty habit of picking up other papers accidentally, and split pins often have vicious points to them. If you insist on using some kind of fastening, perhaps the best way is to use staples – just one staple in the top left-hand corner is adequate, rather than a series of staples all the way down the side (and don't try to staple too many pages together).

ILLUSTRATIONS
Keep these separate from your typescript, especially if they are photographs. If they are diagrams, you should indicate where they are to go in the text. Photographs will probably be batched together by the publisher, but it is to be hoped that he will consult you about their presentation, so that important ones do not appear as miniatures while those of less account are given full pages. Just as you should keep a copy of your typescript, so you should have copies of your illustrations – any good camera shop will make copies of precious, irreplaceable photographs, and diagrams can be photostatted.

FOOTNOTES
Try to avoid them wherever possible by incorporating the material in the main body of the text. Publishers not only dislike them, because they add considerably to the cost of setting the book in type, but may insist, if there are many of them, that they should appear together at the end of a chapter or at the end of the whole book.

INDEX
If your book requires an index, and you are willing to prepare it yourself (and capable of doing so) – a matter which should be discussed with your publisher at contract stage – you clearly cannot carry out the work until the book has been set in print, so that you can include the right page references. You can, however, if you wish, make an index from your typescript for your own use, if you feel this will simplify your task when the proofs arrive. At submission stage, there is no need to supply this rough draft to the publisher, but it would be useful to indicate approximately how many entries there will be in it, or perhaps how many pages you would expect it to occupy.

Books for Children

In this section we are concerned basically with picture books. All the details given under Books – Fiction and Non-Fiction above apply equally to books for older children, which consist primarily of text.

LAYOUT
Follow the guidelines above as far as the text is concerned, typing it out separately, even if it consists of very few words (unless, of course, you are also providing the lettering, in which case text and illustrations will be integrated), and keeping the illustrations separate. Prepare a 'dummy', that is to say, blank sheets of paper made up like a book on which you indicate where the illustrations and the text will appear. Make sure that you use one of the standard page sizes for this kind of book (find out the usual sizes by looking at what is on offer in your local bookshop).

NUMBER OF PAGES
Books are printed in sections consisting of eight, sixteen or thirty-two pages (small sections of four pages can also be produced, and, on large machines, sixty-four and one hundred and twenty-eight pages can be printed on one sheet of paper). A picture book for children is likely to have a maximum of thirty-two pages, and quite often the figure is twelve, sixteen or twenty-four. Four of those pages are frequently used as endpapers, which means that nothing can appear on the first and last pages which will be pasted down to secure the binding. You will also need a title page and a biblio page, and your book cannot therefore really begin until page 5 and will have to end on page 14 or 15 if it is a sixteen page book, and on page 22 or 23 if it has twenty-four pages. If you find this difficult to understand, look at published picture books and work out for yourself how they have been physically made up.

Poetry

LAYOUT
It is usual practice not to type poetry in double spacing, but to put it on your page in exactly the form in which you would like to see it printed. Indentations of various lengths, blank lines – any variations you want – should be there for the printer to follow. This applies whether you are preparing a book of your poetry, or

submitting a single poem to a magazine or to one of the small poetry presses.

BOOKS OF POETRY

As explained in the section on illustrated books for children, books are printed in sections, usually of thirty-two pages. This is why you will find that most books you pick up have a total number of pages such as 160, 192, 224, 256 and so on. With a book which consists entirely or very largely of straightforward text, the publisher can juggle with different types and type sizes to make it fit into one of these lengths which is a multiple of thirty-two. The publisher's designer often has less scope with poetry, except, perhaps, by putting more than one poem on a page, which is rarely desirable, especially in recent times when the visual appearance of poems has become much more important. It is not essential to work out exactly how many pages your poems will occupy (if you have too few, the difference may be made up by a more generous allocation of pages to the prelims, or by leaving blank pages in certain places, and if you have too many, the publisher may ask you to drop one or two of them). But do make sure, if you are asking a hardcover publisher to bring out your poems, that there are sufficient to make a collection of reasonable size. If you have too few poems for that, then go to one of the little presses which publish booklets of poetry in paper bindings.

Plays

LAYOUT

Plays are usually presented with the dialogue in single spacing, but with a double space between speeches by different characters. The stage directions are in brackets and underlined, and are included within the speech if they apply only to the character speaking, but are on separate lines in other cases. The names of the characters speaking should be in capitals on the left-hand side, separated from all the dialogue.

These complicated directions will be made clearer by an example:

> (*Gwendolen and Cecily are at the window, looking out into the garden.*)

GWENDOLEN   The fact that they did not follow us at once into the house, as any one else would have done, seem to me to show that they have some sense of shame left.

CECILY   They have been eating muffins. That looks like repentance.

GWENDOLEN   (*After a pause.*) They don't seem to notice us at all. Couldn't you cough?

CECILY   But I haven't got a cough.

GWENDOLEN   They're looking at us. What effrontery!

CECILY   They're approaching. That's very forward of them.

GWENDOLEN   Let us preserve a dignified silence.

CECILY   Certainly. It's the only thing to do now.

(*Enter Jack followed by Algernon. They whistle some dreadful popular air from a British Opera.*)

If you are writing plays for television or radio, it is usual to number each speech in the play, beginning with 1 and continuing all the way through. The numbers are placed just before the names of the characters who are speaking, on the left-hand side. *Writing for the BBC* gives useful advice, and the BBC Radio Drama Department will send you a specimen layout if you write to them, enclosing a large stamped addressed envelope.

Articles and Short Stories

LAYOUT
You should use A4 and double spacing, but it is not necessary to keep strictly to the same number of words per page, and indeed, if there is a convenient paragraph break near the end of the page, stop there and begin the next paragraph on a new page.

Do not put 'overlap words' at the foot of the page, but do put 'more', or 'more follows' or 'm.f.' at the bottom of the page on the right-hand side, except, of course, on the last page, where you can substitute 'ends'.

On the first page of the text you should put the title at the top or one or two spaces down (unless you are submitting your work to American magazines, when it is customary to begin halfway down the page). Do not use capital letters or underline the title – leave the sub-editor to indicate to the printer how it should appear.

PAGE NUMBERING
Number the pages as usual, but always include an identification too. For example: 'NUTS.1, NUTS.2, etc.' or 'Legat.1, Legat.2, etc.'.

TITLE PAGE
In addition to the title, your by-line (name or pseudonym) and your name and address (or agent's address), indicate whether the article is to be illustrated and whether the illustrations are supplied by you or not. A word count should appear, and this should be fairly accurate, without allowing for short lines. If, however, you use the technique described above for calculating wordage (that is, counting short lines as though they were full ones), round the figure up or down to the nearest fifty words.

You should also add 'First British Serial Rights' or 'F.B.S.R.' or 'Single Reproduction Only', to indicate that you are not selling the magazine or newspaper the copyright in your work (which you should never do). 'First British Serial Rights' means that you are offering the magazine or newspaper the opportunity to publish the article or story for the first time in Britain. You will be free to try to sell American or Australian or other overseas rights in the same piece of work, marking it 'First U.S. Serial Rights' or 'First South African Serial Rights' as appropriate. After its publication in Britain, if it is accepted, you may be able to sell 'Second Serial Rights' to other British magazines or newspapers, and the same applies in overseas markets. The term 'Second Serial Rights', incidentally, includes all uses of the article or story after the first one, whether it is being sold for the second, third, fifth or umpteenth time.

8   Selling Your Work

Market Research

One way of deciding where to try to sell your work is to get a copy of *The Writers' and Artists' Yearbook* or of *The Writers' Handbook*, turn to the appropriate section, and choose a publisher because you like the sound of the firm's name, or by sticking a pin in.

It is not the best way. Both the books mentioned are extremely useful and, although they are available in your public library, should be on every writer's bookshelf. They give details of book publishers, magazines, newspapers, outlets for stage plays, radio, television and films, agents, societies, etc., and include articles on subjects of interest to authors. If you study them carefully you may find invaluable advice on where to send your work. But you really need to do more than that.

The idea of undertaking market research before making a submission seems to fill some would-be writers with dismay. They feel that it is very difficult and very time-consuming. The time that it takes will be well spent, because it should prevent the writer from sending work to a totally unsuitable outlet. As for being hard to do, that belief stems simply from ignorance of how to set about it.

Market research is, in fact, extremely simple in essence. It consists of looking (or, in the case of radio, listening) to see what sort of things are accepted and by whom. So you do it in libraries, bookshops, newsagents, the theatre or the cinema, or in your home by listening to the radio or watching television.

MARKET RESEARCH BEFORE YOU BEGIN WRITING
It is often only after a piece is written that the author thinks about market research, but it can also be done in advance and can, indeed, actually inspire the writing. Many authors have achieved considerable success by studying what was already available and then deciding to fill a gap that they could perceive. 'I could write

such-and-such a book for such-and-such a market' – that is an approach which not only makes an acceptance more likely, but may result in a commission simply on the basis of the idea.

MARKET RESEARCH FOR BOOKS

Suppose you have written a biography of an historical figure (and I am assuming that you have the necessary qualifications to do so), and are wondering where to send it. Go to your local library and look on the shelves to see which publishers regularly bring out biographies of that type. Go to your local bookseller and talk to the owner or manager, who, unless you choose a particularly busy time in the shop, will probably be very willing to give you advice. You can also obtain more information about specific publishers by writing to them and asking for their catalogues. Exactly the same procedure applies whether your book is about gardening, or how to write, or any other kind of non-fiction, or whether it is a novel, whatever the genre, or whether it is intended for children.

You need to do this research with a certain amount of depth, so that you make sure that a given publishing house not only brings out books in the broad category in which you are interested, but that its publications are in the same specific mould as your work; you do not want to send a romance in the style of Barbara Cartland to a publisher whose fiction list is extremely highbrow, nor a right-wing political study to a left-wing house. Equally, you must avoid too close a match; a publisher who has just brought out a book on cooking for beginners is unlikely to want another on exactly the same theme, and if a particular house publishes, for instance, a well known author's series of historical novels featuring Charles II, you will only diminish your chances by sending to that publisher your own novel about Charles and Nell Gwyn.

Should you choose a large publisher or a small one? Both have advantages and disadvantages. The large publisher probably produces a wider spectrum of books, so you may stand a better chance of acceptance, but on the other hand the firm receives so many books for consideration that its editors can afford to be choosy; the small publisher is more likely to be hungry for new authors, but is likely to have a much more limited range. The large publisher may well be more efficient, and with a numerous sales force can be expected to achieve reasonably good sales; unless your book is a potential bestseller, however, it is possible that a small house will give you more attention. I remember expressing surprise to the successful novelist John Brophy when he moved from a large publisher to a medium-sized house; he said that he had not been one of the large publisher's top authors, but only in the middle rank, whereas with his new firm, he would be one of their leading writers – 'It's better to be a large fish in a medium-sized pond, than a medium-sized fish in a large pond.'

Make yourself a list of potential publishers for your work, and work your way through it until either you have an acceptance or you decide to give up. But don't give up too easily. Perseverance is a much needed quality for authors – perseverance in completing their work, and perseverance in their attempts to find a publisher for it.

Packagers

A packager is not a publisher. He or she produces books which are then sold in a finished state to a regular publisher, who then publishes and sells them. Most packaged books are lavishly illustrated, usually with a fair amount of colour printing, and they work principally because the packager sells editions in a number of countries and languages, and can therefore build up a substantial print run and produce the copies at a price which the individual publisher would not be able to match. To explain this further: a book illustrated in colour is usually printed in four colours – yellow, blue, red and black; the text usually appears in black; let us suppose that the British packager has sold 10,000 copies to a British publisher, 20,000 to an American house, 10,000 in France, 15,000 in Germany, and 10,000 in Italy, a total of 65,000; it is then possible to print 65,000 copies from the yellow, blue and red plates in one go, making the colour printing comparatively cheap, while the black plate will be a totally new one each time, to accommodate the change of language for the French, German and Italian editions, and will have some minor alterations for the American edition.

Obviously the books which are suitable for this kind of operation have an international appeal. They are mostly devised by the packagers, who approach and commission an author to write the text, usually supplying the accompanying illustrations themselves. However, if you have an idea which you think might interest a packager, it is certainly worth approaching one of those listed in *The Writers' and Artists' Yearbook*.

Articles

If you are hoping to place articles (and this is, incidentally, probably the easiest way to get into print for the first time), then your market research will have to be rather more precise. Whereas the majority of book publishers have a quite wide-ranging list and bring out books which vary in style, length, and the market at which they are aimed, newspapers and magazines tend to be much more limited in their requirements. You need to study the length of the articles they publish, their editorial policies, and, especially the kind of reader for which they cater. You will probably have to check several issues of a magazine to build up a reliable picture of its editorial policy. Do study the advertisements, by the way, for they can provide valuable clues about the age and interests of the readership.

Short Stories

The market for short stories is a diminishing one. It is generally useless to send a single story to a book publisher, and your chances of getting a collection of stories published are pretty small unless you are an established writer with a high literary reputation. Short stories do, however, still get published in magazines and occasionally in newspapers, and careful market research can tell you where your best chances lie. Be careful to get the length right. If you are writing for women's magazines, then not only will you need to have a woman as the central character, but she will have to be of the right age group for the magazine. Similarly, the age group is of prime importance if you are looking at the 'confessions' magazines.

Poetry

It is not easy to get a book of poetry published unless you have already established yourself in the field. If you keep your eyes open, however, you can find nowadays an increasing number of outlets for poetry. Large numbers of so-called 'little presses' have come into existence, primarily for the purpose of publishing new poets who would otherwise not be seen in print, and new literary magazines, which often publish several pages of poetry, constantly appear (and, regrettably, usually disappear again after a few issues). A useful address list of Small Presses and Little Magazines is published by Oriel, 54 Charles Street, Cardiff CF1 4ED.

There are also various less specialized magazines which will sometimes take a poem, especially if it is relevant to the main content of the publication, and local newspapers can sometimes be cajoled into filling a small empty space with a poem. None of the editors concerned will come knocking at your door, but there is nothing to stop you knocking on their doors, and you may well be invited inside, if you do your market research with care.

Radio and Television

Your market research for radio and television in Britain is necessarily restricted by the fact that you have the BBC on one hand, and the independents on the other, and that is all. The BBC publishes a booklet, *Writing for the BBC*, which tells you exactly what they want and how to set about selling it to them. Their requirements are very similar to those of the independent radio and television organizations. But yet again, the key to success in these fields depends on listening and watching to find out all you need to know about the requisite length of an item, what can and what can't be done effectively in these media, and what sort of content is likely to appeal. There is a strong belief that a kind of 'closed shop' exists for writers in television, and that it is therefore impossible for newcomers to break in. This is not so, but the belief survives partly because so many would-be writers are rejected not because they are newcomers, but because they have not done sufficient market research to ensure that their material is the kind of thing that contemporary television directors are looking for.

Stage Plays

If you want to be a successful dramatist you must study what is happening today in the theatre. Far too many amateur playwrights are producing plays which are old-fashioned in construction, in theme, in setting. Even among the amateurs, who, generally speaking, tend to lag behind the professional theatre in their acceptance of change, the 'well-made play', with its three acts, drawing-room setting and middle-class values, is less popular than it used to be. Nevertheless, it should be remembered that the amateur market is an important one, and not all the plays published by a number of firms (notably, of course, Samuel French Ltd) have previously received professional performances. This is particularly true of the one-act play, still very popular with amateurs, although rarely seen in the professional theatre. But if you want to write for the amateur market, then you must find out what the average local society wants to do and is capable of doing.

Overseas Markets

Market research in the USA, Australia, and other overseas territories may be very difficult for the British writer unless he or she is fortunate enough to travel to faraway places and thus to be able to conduct the necessary research on the ground. This is a pity, especially for the writer of articles or short stories, since there are many lucrative opportunities for this kind of material, especially in the United States. The American *Writer's Market*, available in the United Kingdom, may seem pricey, but is valuable in the detail it provides about American book and magazine publishers. *The Writers' and Artists' Yearbook* also gives useful information about English language markets overseas. Nothing, however, can replace direct study of any publications for which you hope to write, and it is well worth the trouble of getting hold of them if you possibly can.

The sale of overseas rights in books and, indeed, almost any literary form other than articles and short stories, is probably best left in the hands of an agent, if you have one, or the British publisher or other licensee of the rights in the material.

Agents

Although you will always need to do a certain amount of market research – at least to the extent of keeping yourself abreast of modern styles and trends – an agent can save you most of the chores which we have so far been discussing in this chapter. A substantial part of a literary agent's job is, in fact, market research. He or she must be constantly knowledgeable about where to send a client's work with the best chance of success, and will also always be looking for opportunities to bring publishers and authors together for the commissioning of new work. The same applies, of course, if the agent is one who specializes in work for the theatre, or radio or television.

Good agents have other extremely useful functions:

1. They will ensure that your contract is a fair one, and will often be able to get more money for your work than you would if you were negotiating on your own. This is not to say either that unless you have an agent most publishers will cheat you badly, or

that having an agent will transform you from a poor writer into a rich one. Some rogue publishers do exist, and if you have an agent, he or she will certainly save you from the clutches of such firms, but if you are on your own, you will be reasonably safe with any of the well-established companies (you can judge them, by the way, by the authors they already publish – if they have some well-known writers on the list you can be fairly sure that such people would not stay with a cheating publisher). As for becoming rich, all that an agent can normally do is to improve the terms of your contract to a comparatively small extent, and whether or not you become rich depends on whether or not you write the kind of books which have the qualities to become bestsellers.

2. An agent will be your watchdog, making sure that the publisher fulfils the terms of the contract (and that includes checking royalty statements for accuracy), and will also conduct any disputes that you may have with your publisher. This last can be very useful, because it saves you from having a personal row, which you may find embarrassing, and moreover the agent will know exactly how justified your complaint is and how far to go in the argument with the publisher without endangering the publisher's commitment to you.

3. An agent will try to retain most subsidiary rights in your work so that they remain in your control, and will then make all possible efforts to sell them on your behalf.

4. An agent will read your work with care, and will often be prepared to offer editorial advice.

5. One of the principal things that a good agent offers is friendship. Many authors regard their publishers as enemies, but even in those cases where author and publisher appear to be on good terms, there is usually some conflict of interest lurking beneath the surface, and a certain wariness behind the bonhomie. Of course the relationship between an author and his agent may not always be all sweetness and light – hence the story of the author whose will left instructions that he was to be cremated, and ten per cent of his ashes scattered over his agent – but in general the agent is on the author's side, and is a good, sympathetic friend and adviser, practised in the provision of a shoulder to cry on, ready to give encouragement, and always conscious that his or her client is a person, rather than an inhuman writing machine.

Most would-be authors, trying to get into print, have the impression that it is almost impossible to do so without an agent. That is not true. It certainly does not apply if you confine yourself to the writing of articles (with the sale of which most agents do not involve themselves) or of short stories (which most agents handle only for their established clients). Nevertheless, an agent is undoubtedly going to help you considerably – publishers do not buy only from agents, but they do look especially carefully at agented work, because they know that the agent would not be handling it if it did not have a modicum of merit, and would probably not have sent it to them if it were unsuitable for their list.

WHAT DOES AN AGENT COST?
Most agents charge ten per cent of any moneys earned from the literary work of their clients. The deduction may rise to nineteen or twenty per cent in respect of foreign sales, because two agents are involved – your own, and your agent's representative in the foreign country concerned. Agents do not normally take any fees until money has actually come in in respect of your work. Therefore, if their efforts to place it should fail, they will not charge you a fee to cover the expenses in which they have been involved. A few agents ask for fifteen per cent of earnings, and some charge a reading fee for unsolicited typescripts.

You also have some responsibilities towards an agent once you have been taken on as a client. Firstly, you should be prepared to give your agent your trust – it is his or her business to know what the going rates are, what is reasonable and what is not, how long to continue trying to place a typescript, and so on. The agent is a professional, and you should accept the advice you are given. Secondly, it is conventionally accepted that, unless it is agreed otherwise, you should involve your agent and pay the normal percentage on work which you have found for yourself as opposed to work which your agent has found for you.

Of course, you may come to the conclusion that, professional or not, the agent's advice and the effort made on your behalf are not what you had hoped for, or that you are obtaining all your work yourself, and therefore deriving no benefit from the agent. There is no contract between authors and agents, so you are free to leave at any time, either to find another agent or to work independently from that time on. Another convention dictates, however, that, unless specifically agreed otherwise, any work originally handled by an agent should remain in that agent's control, at least until the work goes out of print, and that he or she should continue to take the standard cut of moneys received in respect of the work.

HOW TO GET AN AGENT
Ay, there's the rub! It is even more difficult to find an agent than to

find a publisher. To begin with, there are fewer agents – the listings for United Kingdom firms in *The Writers' and Artists' Yearbook* cover some dozen pages, whereas British book publishers take up four times as much space. Secondly, agents are involved in considerable expenses – they have staff to pay and offices to maintain, as well the cost of correspondence and the sending out of typescripts – and one agent has recently gone on record as saying that he can only make a profit out of clients who can be relied upon to make £20,000 a year from their writing (of which his cut would be £2,000). That is undoubtedly a high figure, but most agents would agree that when they take on a new client they are hoping for that author to be making, within a comparatively short period, a minimum of £5,000 a year from writing alone. Thirdly, since the relationship between an author and an agent is a very personal one, you need to find someone who is compatible with you (and if you do get an offer from an agent to take you on, the first thing to do is to arrange a meeting so that you can assure yourself that you have indeed found a friend as well as a business partner).

So it is difficult to get an agent. One possibility is to try some of the smaller, newer firms, who are more likely to be looking for clients. Another is to approach an agent once you have interested a publisher in your work – that is to say, when you have received the offer of a contract, but before you have actually signed it. An agent may be much more willing to take you on at that stage, with the guarantee of at least some income from your work.

If you cannot persuade an agent to represent you, do not despair. Very many authors work perfectly happily by direct contact with their publishers, and it has to be said that many publishers often prefer not to have an agent involved – not because they wish to cheat the author, but because if there is no agent, the publisher will usually control all the subsidiary rights, and that will mean not only that he receives some income from their sale but that he has those rights to offer, which gives him status and sometimes bargaining power with, for instance, foreign publishers.

Vanity Publishers

Vanity publishing is a technical term referring to a specific kind of publishing which is based on the author making a substantial contribution towards the production costs of the book, with the assurance that, when sufficient copies of the book have been sold, the money will come back to the author in the form of high royalties. In most cases, the 'contribution' consists of the entire costs, plus the vanity publisher's profit, and despite expansive promises, the book will not achieve a wide bookshop sale, and the author will never get any of his money back.

Vanity publishers are expert at flattering authors who have failed to get their books accepted by regular publishing houses, and at giving the impression that the success of the book in question is virtually guaranteed. They are also highly skilled in not saying anything which can later be held against them, and their contracts are usually watertight and contain no clauses which they do not fulfil. There is, in fact, nothing illegal about vanity publishing.

It has to be admitted that vanity publishers usually take considerable pains to ensure that the books which they produce are attractive in appearance. It is, however, an extremely expensive, and in the long run disappointing, way of getting into print, and you are strongly advised against it. There are some occasions when regular publishers accept contributions from an author towards production costs, but if you are ever offered a publishing contract which does include such a contribution, you should check carefully and take advice before signing.

If you have failed to interest a regular publisher in your work, and you have a little money which you wish to spend on putting the work into print, then the answer is to go to a printer (or even a printshop – at least make an enquiry there first) and pay the firm to produce copies for you. You should get an estimate first – preferably several estimates, from which you can make a choice. There are books available which will tell you exactly how to go about it, including such mysteries as the need for an ISBN and how you obtain one – *How to Publish Yourself* by Peter Finch is a helpful example. The point of doing it yourself in this way is that you will have all the expense, but you will also pocket all the receipts from sales of your book. However, it has to be said that comparatively few authors who publish their own work succeed in marketing it adequately – established publishers often experience difficulty in getting widespread distribution of their books, and it is obviously even harder for the author working on his or her own. But it can be done, and has been done – principally with books which really do supply a gap in the market.

Submissions

BOOKS

When you have decided where you are going to send your work it is advisable to write first to ask whether you may submit it for consideration. Apart from anything else, if your typescript is bulky it will save the cost of mailing it to a publisher or agent who might not be interested in it. It is worth phoning first to find out the name (and how it is spelt) of the chief editor or editorial director or the member of the agency who deals with that kind of work, so that you can write to him or her personally. Your letter should be brief and businesslike, describing the work in a few words which will give a clear indication of its scope, but without going into a long summary. If you have qualifications for writing it, mention them. There is no point in saying that your friends enjoyed the work, because the editor or agent does not know their critical abilities and will suspect that in any case they would not have dared to tell you if they didn't like it; on the other hand, if the typescript has been read and admired by a well-known personality or an authority in the field, you should certainly include that information. Enclose a stamped addressed envelope for the reply.

If you receive a favourable answer, mail or deliver the work, enclosing return postage. If you deliver by hand, do not expect to talk to the editor or agent – your work must speak for itself, and any essential information (such as the fact that you can supply additional illustrations if required) can be included in your covering letter.

Then be patient. Few publishers will give you a verdict in less than three weeks, and very often there is a much longer delay. If you have not heard after three months, you can send a polite inquiry; after six months without response, you are entitled to write a strongly worded letter, asking for your typescript to be returned. You will lose nothing by showing your anger at this stage – if you have heard nothing for that long, it is unlikely that the firm in question is interested in your work, and its behaviour will have been reprehensible.

SUBMITTING A SYNOPSIS

One way of cutting down on the time that publishers take to consider a typescript (and also of saving considerably on postage) is to send a synopsis of your work and a specimen chapter or two rather than the whole thing. This is quite a good idea for non-fiction (see the section on Commissions below), but may not work so well with fiction. Most, but not all, publishers prefer to see a complete novel, because it is often very difficult to decide from the sight of a single chapter, or even two, how effectively the story will be written. However, you will probably lose very little by trying. Before sending it off, it would certainly be worth asking your chosen publishers whether they would be prepared to consider your work in that form.

MULTIPLE SUBMISSIONS

Another possibility is to send your work to more than one house simultaneously. Is this allowed? Some publishers object to the practice, but many others are willing to tolerate it. You could ask in your preliminary letter whether the publisher would mind if you showed the typescript elsewhere at the same time.

POETRY

If you hope to get your poetry published in one of the little magazines, you can probably risk sending your work off without first seeking the magazine's permission, but you will of course enclose a short covering note and a stamped addressed envelope if you want your material returned. It is best to send no more than three of your poems for consideration. If the editor likes your work, he or she will probably ask to see more.

ARTICLES

If you have done your market research carefully and therefore have a good idea that your work will be of interest to a certain magazine or newspaper, you can submit your work 'on spec', without writing first. If, however, you make a preliminary enquiry and get a favourable response, you will at least have the certainty that your work will be looked at with interest. It is worth remembering, by the way, that most magazines work some way ahead, and if your article is intended, for instance, for a Christmas issue, it needs to be submitted in the previous August. If it is immediately topical, you will have very little chance of acceptance unless it is also a subject of continuing interest. For further information on the submission of articles, see *The Way to Write Magazine Articles* by John Hines, which is the best of the several good handbooks available.

SHORT STORIES

The remarks above on articles also apply to short stories, but since the outlets are comparatively few, market research is even more essential. Donna Baker's book, *How to Write Stories for Magazines* is very helpful.

PLAYS

Plays can be sent to theatre managements, or even to a leading actor for whom you have written a star part, but your best approach is probably through one of the agents who specialize in handling dramatic work. If your work is intended only for the amateur theatre, it can be submitted in the normal way to one of the publishing houses which caters for this market.

Commissions

Unless you are a well-established author you are unlikely to be commissioned to write a work of fiction. As already explained, if you send no more than a specimen chapter or two and a synopsis of a novel, most publishers will not go beyond an expression of interest in seeing the completed work in due course. There are, however, some exceptions to this rule, notably Mills & Boon.

With non-fiction, on the other hand, the submission of a detailed synopsis and specimen chapters stands much more chance of resulting in a commission and a contract. This is especially true if your work is of an original nature, if you can demonstrate that you have good qualifications for writing it, and if you have done your market research well and can show the publisher that no other book covering the same ground is already available. For more details on how to go about it, see *The Successful Author's Handbook* by Gordon Wells, which can be warmly recommended.

Rejections

Never despair if your work is rejected. There are dozens of reasons why a piece of writing is not accepted, and many of them have nothing to do with the quality of the piece. The person to whom you send it may just have taken on a very similar work, or may have so crowded a publication schedule that there is no room for additions, or, despite your careful market research, the editorial policy may have changed. Moreover, editors are human beings, with personal likes and dislikes, and good and bad moods, and it may be simply that your work has been looked at by someone who is out of sympathy with it, and that the next editor to see it will jump at it. Keep on trying. Remember the many stories of famous authors who have struggled for years before getting a book accepted, and have then immediately shot on to the bestseller list with it. Of course, if you receive a whole series of rejections, you should perhaps begin to wonder whether the quality of the writing is at fault, especially if you have not received any kind word from any of the editors who have seen it.

If you do receive a rejection which also contains some praise, and perhaps even a request to see anything else that you write, you can really feel encouraged. Publishers are not in the habit of writing in that vein unless they mean it.

Don't expect a rejection to include detailed criticism of your work. A few publishers will take the trouble to explain why they are turning something down, but most of them say that if they were to write lengthy, explanatory rejection letters, they would not have enough time to work on the books that they were accepting.

The Rights Offered

There is considerable confusion about 'First British Serial Rights', a phrase which many beginners believe they should type on the front of any work they produce. It should appear on work submitted to a magazine or newspaper (see p.111), but in the case of a book which you are offering directly to a publisher, what you are hoping to sell is 'Volume Rights', and indeed, the publisher will probably ask, if accepting the book, simply for 'World Rights'. The copyright will remain with you, but the publisher will have the right to grant licences for the use of the book in dozens of different ways, including U.S. and foreign rights, paperback, book club, film, radio, anthology and many other rights, sharing the proceeds with you in agreed proportions as laid down in the contract between you.

Keeping a Copy

Never ever send out your work without keeping a copy. The majority of publishers will take reasonable care of your typescript and return it, if it is rejected, but there are inevitable cases when the material is lost, and it is normal practice that work is submitted at the author's risk, so if your work does go walkabout, there will be no compensation. Parcels also sometimes go astray in the post. So always keep a copy. Some authors, when submitting articles, stories or poems will say in the covering letter that they do not expect the material to be returned if it is not accepted, but of course they can only do that if they are secure in the knowledge of being able to produce a second copy if need be. If you work on a word processor, you may feel that it is sufficient to keep your work filed on disc, but it is well worth printing out a second copy for yourself, because discs can occasionally become defective, quite apart from the hazard of accidental erasure.

9   Libel and Other Legal Problems

Before you send your work to a publisher, it is as well to feel easy in your mind as far as the legality of its content is concerned. If it is a book and it is accepted for publication you will almost certainly have to sign a warranty that it is free from unlawful material.

In the case of several of the offences listed in this chapter, such as obscene libel, blasphemous libel and sedition, the author will be fully aware of the risks he or she is taking. But many beginners worry over libel, which is probably the commonest cause for legal action as far as authors are concerned, and some appear to be quite unaware that plagiarism is a punishable sin.

Libel

If you publish something which damages someone's reputation in the eyes of other people you have perpetrated a libel, and may be sued.

The first thing to make clear is that you do not commit libel if you write in complimentary or even neutral terms about another person, unless your tone is so heavily ironic that you are clearly intending the opposite of the face value of the words. An essential quality of libel is that it is always damaging.

Secondly, you cannot libel the dead, although you must beware of making a statement about a dead person which might seriously affect the reputations of his or her descendants.

If you are writing non-fiction, the issues are usually clear-cut. A statement in a book or article which accuses a named person of criminal activity or of socially unacceptable behaviour can be very dangerous, unless you can prove that the facts you have presented are true (and preferably, widely known to be true).

'Justification' – that is to say that you have merely printed the truth – is the first and best defence against a threat of libel.

You may wonder how journalists get away with saying, for

instance, that the leader of a political party is an incompetent fool. The defence in this case would be that the statement is 'fair comment' – a matter of opinion, rather than of fact, stated in good faith and without malice. In any case, politicians, and indeed many public figures, are commonly treated in this way, and would spend their lives in litigation if they really believed that such comments were harmful to them. On the other hand, if you say that a politician has misappropriated moneys, for instance, you will be in trouble. Equally, your defence of 'fair comment' might be less easy to sustain if you had said in print that the managing director of a small firm was an incompetent fool. Although not necessarily nationally known, such a person would probably be very dependent on the good opinion of his customers, and might find your comment extremely damaging. To make matters worse, you could well have some difficulty in proving that your statement was true, in order to plead 'justification'.

A third defence against a libel action is 'privilege'. This applies chiefly to reports of judicial and parliamentary proceedings, and of public meetings, provided that the report is fair and accurate.

Before you include any potentially libellous material in your writing, do be certain that it is essential for your purposes. Even if you are sure that you would win any libel case brought against you, a court action is always extremely expensive, in time as well as in money. If you are doubtful about whether something you have written is libellous, always tell your publisher about it. He or she may take legal advice on the matter, but in any case it is your duty to make it clear that a risk exists.

The problems for fiction writers are considerable. You will no doubt have seen those notices which publishers often place at the beginning of novels – 'All of the characters in this book are fictitious, and any resemblance to actual persons, living or dead, is purely coincidental'. Such a notice may help to deter a frivolous litigant, but is basically worthless, and will not protect either the author or the publisher if the book does in fact contain libellous material.

It is always risky to portray characters from life if you are describing those persons and their actions as discreditable. You can give the characters different names, and it may help to change their physical appearance and circumstances. Nevertheless, if any of the persons concerned, and especially their friends and acquaintances, can recognize them as the originals of your characters, there will be the possibility of a case of libel.

You must also be careful in fiction to avoid using the real name of a professional person, such as a doctor or a lawyer, if you are going to ascribe unethical actions to the character concerned. If, for instance, you invent a doctor who is peddling illegal drugs, and you give him the name of a real-life doctor, you can be in serious trouble. A defence does exist on the grounds of 'innocence' – that is to say, you had no knowledge of the libelled person's existence, had no malicious intent, and used his or her name by accident, as it were. But that is a difficult defence to invoke, and in a situation like that it is worth consulting the BMA list of doctors to ensure that you choose a name which does not appear on it.

If a libel case is brought against something that you have written, the ultimate responsibility is yours. In theory, at least, you will have to pay all damages and costs awarded in the case, and the cost of the defence. In practice, your publishers may agree to share such costs, especially if you have warned them of the possibility of libel and they have agreed to take the risk of prosecution. It's far better to avoid the problem altogether, if you possibly can.

Plagiarism

Plagiarism is the deliberate copying of another author's work without either permission or even acknowledgment. You are permitted to quote small portions of someone else's published material under the convention of 'fair usage' – that is to say, the quoted material is used briefly, for instance, to support your own argument, or to illustrate a point. Such a quotation should always be acknowledged by the inclusion of the author's name, the title of the work from which it comes, and preferably its publisher too. If the passage to be quoted is at all lengthy, you should seek permission to use it, and pay any appropriate fee. By convention, however, you are free to quote a reasonable amount of material (say, up to 400 words) from a book in a review of it that you write.

But, apart from direct quotation, what about a more general use of another author's material? Supposing you are writing a non-fiction book on a certain subject; you will almost certainly read a large number of other books on the same subject. Can you be accused of plagiarism if your book contains similar material to those you have read? Generally speaking, no. Make sure, however, that everything you write is in your own words, and that you acknowledge the source of any specific material which is not a generally known fact. It is also advisable to avoid copying the exact arrangement of the material in a way which would suggest that you had taken someone else's work as a direct model.

What about plots in fiction? It is well known that the number of basic plots is limited to a handful, so can you be accused of plagiarism if your plot is similar to that of another author? It depends on the degree of similarity. If your story follows all the twists and turns of an existing work of fiction, with the same cast of characters, even if they have different names and perhaps a different setting, you would indeed be stealing (which is what plagiarism is). Your only defence would be to prove that you were totally unaware of the previously published book, and you might find it very difficult to do so.

Obscenity

You might think that nowadays there is no risk of prosecution for obscenity. It is certainly difficult to imagine any non-fiction being taken to court for this reason, as manuals on birth control were in the past, though perhaps in the field of autobiography it might be possible. Four-letter words and detailed descriptions of the sexual act are commonplace in published fiction, and there appear to be no limits. However, blatant pornography is still liable to prosecution, and the police still raid bookshops which deal in this trade (often including in their nets a number of books generally considered to be respectable).

The problem is that the borderline between pornographic writing and what is permissible is very vague – lawyers have struggled for years and in vain to produce a really satisfactory definition of pornography. Who can say with certainty that this piece of writing will 'deprave and corrupt' the average person, and who is the average person anyway? We all have our own standards in making this kind of judgment. Literary quality can be cited in evidence in obscenity trials, and it seems fair to say that the author's intention is of paramount importance – is the material in question an integral and essential part of the writing, placed there for serious literary reasons, or has it been inserted gratuitously, not merely to titillate, but indeed to deprave and corrupt? And that, of course, brings us back to the insoluble problem of deciding what is no more than acceptable titillation, and what is something a great deal worse.

Blasphemous Libel

Blasphemous libel, in Britain, is concerned with offensive material about the Christian religion, but in our multi-racial society, it is possible that a prosecution in respect of another religion might be successful, and, indeed, there is a move afoot to change the present law to protect the religious susceptibilities of non-Christians. As with obscene libel, it is difficult to define exactly what constitutes blasphemous libel. There is no illegality in any anti-religious writings which are serious in tone and moderate in language and approach. To be libellous in this sense the material must be of a truly outrageous nature, and will probably be obscene as well as blasphemous.

Racism

It is an offence to publish racially offensive material, for which you can be prosecuted under the Race Relations Act, especially if your aim is clearly to stir up racial hatred. Comparatively few writers will go that far, but it is as well to avoid any racist attitude which, even if not so blatant as to risk prosecution, could give offence. This is especially important for the writers of children's books (who have also, of course, to beware of sexism).

Sedition

Writings which aim to destroy the peace of the realm by violent means are subject to prosecution. Under this heading may also be included works which breach confidentiality, as instanced in the recent *Spycatcher* case, or remembering the furore which was caused some forty years ago when 'Crawfie', governess to the Princesses Elizabeth and Margaret Rose, published her memoirs. Prosecutions are rare, and the authors of such books frequently appear to benefit enormously from the publicity which is generated by attempts to ban their works. Presumably they are little troubled by conscience as they bank the proceeds.

Passing Off

There is no copyright in titles, and you are therefore free to call your work by any name you like. However, if you choose a title which is already a household word, you risk being prosecuted by the author or owner of the copyright of the original work for 'passing off' – that is to say, you will be accused of trying to persuade the public to buy your book under the impression that it is the famous one. Some titles appear quite often on different books, but should not be used if they have already been appropriated for a bestseller. So if you want to call your book *From Russia with Love* or *The Kon-Tiki Expedition* or *Gone with the Wind*, think again.

Equally, there is no copyright in authors' names, but however unfair it may seem, if your name happens to be the same as that of some famous contemporary writer, you will probably be well advised to use a pseudonym, if only to avoid confusion.

10   Payment For Your Work

The Publisher's First Offer

If a book publisher to whom you have sent your work decides to accept it for publication, you will almost certainly receive a letter containing an offer (unless the publisher wants you to do a considerable amount of revision before reaching that stage). The letter will not go into a great deal of detail, which will be left until contract stage, but will probably name a sum as the advance to be paid against the book's earnings, will specify the instalments in which that advance is to be paid, and will list the royalties payable on ordinary sales of the publisher's edition of the book in the domestic market and overseas.

The first thing to remember is that hardly any authors make enough from their writing to live on, so the amounts offered will not stagger you by their enormous size. Indeed, in certain fields, such as 'library fiction' (romantic novels, westerns and similar genre books which sell principally to libraries rather than in bookshops), the publisher is in a buyer's market, able to choose from dozens of submitted books of almost equal standard, and therefore the offer may indeed stagger you – but by its minuscule size.

The second point to remember is that the offer is not necessarily a final one. If the publisher has got as far as making an offer for the book, a fair amount of time has already been spent on it, and he or she actually wants to publish it, and may already have slotted it in tentatively to the publishing schedule. You are unlikely, therefore, to have the offer withdrawn if you dare to query its terms and ask for them to be improved. Don't, however, especially if this is your first book, expect more than a modest improvement, and be prepared for the publisher to refuse the request altogether.

You may be particularly ready to ask for an increase in the size of the advance. After all, it is guaranteed money, and you may feel too that the larger the advance, the more effort the publisher will put into the publication. The advances which publishers offer are calculated in rough proportion to the sales they envisage, including possibly the sale of subsidiary rights, and a book with a five figure advance carries greater expectations and is inevitably going to get more attention than one for which the publisher has put down, say, £500. But the difference in effort on a book for which the advance is £750 rather than £500 is minimal. Get an increase if you can, but since, if the publisher has offered a modest advance, you are unlikely to be able to pressure him or her into an astronomic figure, you will probably do better to try to increase the royalties. Royalties are, of course, birds in the bush, while the advance is a bird in the hand, but the higher the royalties the sooner the advance will be earned, and your long term benefits may be much greater if you secure an improvement in that field.

Copyright

Copyright exists in a work as soon as it is written, and normally extends, in respect of works published during the author's lifetime, for fifty years after his or her death.

You should always retain your copyright in your work. Most book publishers' contracts take the form of a licence, in which you give the publisher various rights in return for specified payments, but they do not usually entail the surrender of your copyright. Look askance at any offer, and especially any contract, which requires you to do so. It is not simply a matter of principle, but of hard commercial fact. If you abandon your copyright, the publisher who owns it may exploit your work in any way, possibly selling hundreds of thousands of copies of your work over a long period without paying you a single penny more.

There may, nevertheless, be certain extraordinary circumstances in which you could be tempted to sell your copyright, doing so with a fair amount of equanimity. One is if you are offered a really substantial sum of money for it, especially if you are in need of the immediate cash; but do think twice, for if the publisher is willing to lay out a big sum of money, the odds are that he expects to get it back tenfold, and you would do much better on a royalty. The only other reason I can think of for giving up your basic ownership of your work is if the publisher, when about to commission a book, threatens to give the job to someone else if you won't agree to surrender your copyright, and tells you, moreover, that he knows half a dozen competent authors who would be only too happy to sign a contract on those terms; it is very hard, for the sake of a principle, to give up a commission of that sort, and the certainty both of payment and publication. An author I know was commissioned to write a short book for a publisher who offered an outright fee for the copyright. When my friend protested, the publisher refused to alter his offer. The author, who was eighty-seven at the time, said to herself, 'If I insist on a royalty I may die before the book actually earns anything. The amount offered isn't bad, and if I take it now I shall have the benefit of it while I'm still able to enjoy it.' She took the money, and enjoyed it, and although she is still alive and might have earned a larger sum in royalties than she was paid, she does not regret her decision. If I live to be eighty-seven and am still writing, I might follow her example. Meanwhile, however, no.

Newspapers and magazines often attempt to purloin an author's copyright. In payment for the work some will send a cheque which requires to be receipted on the back, but the wording above the space for the author's signature grants the paper or magazine copyright in the piece. If you get a cheque like that, cross out the reference to copyright and initial the deletion before signing.

The Publisher's Contract

Following your acceptance of the basic terms offered by the publisher, a contract will, in due course, make its appearance. It is likely to be a document of formidable length and complexity, reflecting not only the many ramifications of the book business today, but also the modern need to specify in some detail the rights and duties of both parties. Many of those clauses and sub-clauses are there because neither publishers nor authors can always be relied on nowadays to behave in an honourable way without the constraint provided by a legal document. But in case you think I have in mind the 'good old days', when a handshake between publisher and author was sufficient to cover all eventualities to the satisfaction of both parties, let me hasten to add that there has never been such a time. Authors and publishers have always been in conflict, and always will be. To listen to or read articles by the more militant of today's authors, you might think that publishers have become much more villainous in recent times, and authors much more hard done by. Not so. What has changed is that the period following the Second World War has seen a previously unknown willingness of authors to air their mostly justified grievances against publishers and to campaign jointly for better terms. In fact, you are much better off with that long and complicated contract than you would have been in the days of nothing more than an apparently friendly handshake.

However, the document is indeed long and complex. Don't sign it without reading it carefully. Even if you have an agent whom you trust and the contract has been drawn up by him or her rather than by the publisher (most agents have their own agreement forms), you should still read it before signing.

If you do not have an agent, you will probably need to do more than read it. You will need advice. The book concerned could turn into a bestseller, or at least one which will continue to provide you with a substantial income for many years to come. Unlikely? Then think of a book such as *Jonathan Livingstone Seagull*, which was a failure when it first appeared, and then suddenly became a cult bestseller around the world. You should never count on miracles, but they do occasionally happen. So this contract could end up being more important to you than those you sign when you buy a house.

The cheapest advice you can get is probably from a friend who is a published author – perhaps someone you have met at a writers' circle. Such people can be knowledgeable and helpful, but quite often their experience of publishers' contracts is limited, so this cheap advice may not really be adequate.

You could go, as you would over the purchase of a house, to a solicitor. You do need, however, to engage the services of a firm which deals regularly with the book world and authors' contracts. Your local solicitor will understand the legal side of a publisher's contract, but is quite unlikely to appreciate fully how the book trade works, and will probably not know what is standard practice, nor see some of the implications of certain clauses. The problem is that, while expert legal advice is readily available, it is expensive.

The next possibility is to join the Society of Authors, which you are eligible to do as soon as you have a firm offer from a publisher. Or you could join the Writers' Guild of Great Britain. Both organizations are equipped to give their members free and reliable guidance on contracts.

Failing all else, you could do worse than to buy a copy of my book *An Author's Guide to Publishing*, and study the chapter on contracts. I say that without any lack of modesty simply because the chapter contains the full text of the Minimum Terms Agreement (see below), together with comments on it. The chapter will tell you a great deal about what you should expect to see in your contract, and what alterations to fight for.

The Minimum Terms Agreement

There is nothing standard about book publishers' contracts – each firm has its own form of contract, and so does each agent, and the terms and conditions vary very widely. In 1981 the Society of Authors and the Writers' Guild presented to the Publishers Association a document known as the Minimum Terms Agreement, which they had drawn up jointly. The MTA laid down the basic terms which, the Society and the Guild suggested, would be acceptable to their members, and the hope was that the substantial changes which it proposed should become standard throughout the industry.

The Publishers Association, on the grounds that it cannot make binding agreements on behalf of its members, refused to endorse the MTA; instead, it produced a bland Code of Practice to which its members may or may not adhere. The Society and the Guild were then forced to approach individual publishers, and try to persuade them to accept the agreement. Progress has been lamentably slow, and at the time of writing less than a dozen firms have signed. However, the pace of recruiting appears to have speeded up recently, and it can also be seen that the mere existence of the MTA has led some other publishers to make (mostly minor) improvements to the terms of their contracts. Many, however, still look upon the MTA as an arm of the Devil, designed to bring publishers to despair and ruin.

Since all publishers have their own little quirks, the MTAs which have been signed differ in certain clauses; additionally, since 1981 the MTA has been amended by the Society and the Guild to remove some of the points which they have been forced to admit were too contentious. Nevertheless, the two main principles remain: a reasonable sharing between author and publisher of the financial rewards, especially if the book is successful, and the recognition that the author should be regarded by the publisher as a partner, to be consulted and kept informed concerning the publication of the book. The present signatories of the MTA accepted these principles willingly, and it is to be hoped that more and more publishers will adopt them as time goes by.

Many authors feel that the second point is the more important; they are tired of being treated condescendingly by publishers, some of whom seem to feel that the author's part in the publication of a book should finish as soon as he or she has completed the typescript, and who take the attitude that any author is lucky to be published, and should, like small Victorian children, be seen and not heard (and preferably not seen either).

A few of the important points in the MTA are:

LICENCE

The majority of publishers will expect to have a licence for the full period of copyright, but it is becoming increasingly common to put a shorter term to the licence, such as ten or fifteen years, after which a new contract can be negotiated, or the rights may revert to the author. There should also be adequate provision for the reversion of rights to the author if the work becomes out of print or if the publisher fails in various respects to adhere to the terms of the contract.

ADVANCE

The advance which a publisher pays is normally non-returnable. It is set against all earnings, such as royalties and income from subsidiary rights, which means that you do not get any further payment until the advance has been earned.

The advance is usually paid either in two instalments (on signature of the agreement if the book has already been delivered, and on publication), or in three instalments (on signature of the agreement, on delivery of the typescript, and on publication). Publication should not normally be delayed for more than twelve months after delivery of the typescript, and you should ask for the final part of the advance to be paid 'on publication or one year after delivery of the typescript, whichever is the sooner'. If you have not delivered the typescript when the agreement is signed, do not accept a clause which says that the next instalment of the advance will be paid 'on acceptance' of the work by the publisher – that, in effect, means that all the publisher has agreed to do is to consider your completed work for publication, and it leaves him or her free to reject it at that stage.

ROYALTIES

Except in some cases, such as highly illustrated books for which the author does not supply the illustrations, the standard royalties are 10% of the retail price on sales in the domestic market, and 10% of the publisher's receipts on sales in the export market. Both rates should rise to 12½% after the sale of 2,500 copies in the respective markets, and to 15% after a further sale of 2,500 copies. You may have to be content with a less favourable rising scale, but always aim at these breaks.

ALTERATIONS
No alterations should be made to the typescript without the knowledge and approval of the author.

CONSULTATION
While the publisher retains control of the production of the book, the author should be consulted about the blurb, the jacket design, the review list and the date of publication.

AUTHOR'S COPIES
For years it has been standard for authors to receive six free copies of the published book. Ask for ten, or, if the book is a mass paperback, for twenty.

SUBSIDIARY RIGHTS
These include rights sold to a mass paperback house, to a book club, to U.S. and foreign publishers, serial, radio, television, tape, disc, dramatization, digest, merchandizing, anthology and quotation, and picture book rights. All other rights should be reserved by you.

As examples, you should look for the following shares of subsidiary rights income: mass paperbacks – 60%, rising to 70% after the first 50,000 copies; U.S. rights – 85%, or if the publisher sells copies of the book to an American publisher on a royalty-inclusive basis, 20% of receipts; first serial rights – 90%; second serial rights – 75%; translation rights – 80%; book club rights – 10% of the price received by the publisher on the first 10,000 copies, and 12½% thereafter, if the publisher sells copies to the book club at a price inclusive of royalties, but if the arrangement is subject to a royalty paid by the book club on its sales, the author's share of royalties should start at 60% and rise to 70% at a point to be agreed.

Although royalties on the publisher's own editions of the book are normally paid at six-monthly intervals, any moneys received by the publisher from sub-contractors, and amounting to £100 or more, should be paid to the author within one month of receipt by the publisher, provided that the advance has been earned.

ILLUSTRATIONS, QUOTATIONS, INDEX
The agreement should contain clear statements as to whether the author or the publisher is responsible for the provision of these and for any payment involved in the clearance of rights. In some cases payment may be shared between the author and the publisher.

OPTIONS

The MTA does not include an option clause giving the publisher the right to sign up the author's next work or works. You should not sign such a clause. If the publisher insists that you do so, at least never accept a wording to the effect that the publisher has the right to buy a subsequent work on the same terms as the contract you are signing – insist that it should be 'on terms to be agreed'.

The exclusion of an option clause does not mean that an author should not submit a new book to his existing publisher, but only that there is no legal commitment to do so. Publishers prize loyalty in their authors, and authors should be happy to demonstrate it – but only if they are satisfied with the treatment they have received.

Please note that the points above are not all those covered by the MTA, and let me emphasize again the value, if you do not have an agent, of joining one of the authors' organizations (see p.155) once an offer is made for your book, since you will be able to obtain detailed advice on the contract from those organizations.

It is also only fair to make it clear that an argument over a contract is a matter of haggling. The publisher is in business to make money; so are you. Both of you will get the best bargain that you can, and that may result in a compromise. Never be afraid to query anything in a publisher's contract before you sign it. As long as you do so courteously, and are prepared to listen to the arguments which the publisher puts forward, there is always the possibility that you will be able to improve the contract from your own point of view. Even if you don't succeed in persuading him or her to give you everything you ask for, you should not sign until you feel you have reached an agreement which is reasonably fair to both sides. To accept poor terms is a disservice not only to yourself, but to all authors.

It is also true that a publisher who presents an author with a manifestly unfair contract, and refuses to improve it, will probably not be a very good publisher anyway – however much you long to be in print, a rejection of the offered agreement may bring you less disappointment in the end. One word of warning, however: before you condemn an agreement as totally unfair, you do need to understand the market situation. Some publishers bring out small editions of books, produced as cheaply as possible, in order to fill a specific market requirement. Their contracts may not meet the requirements of the MTA, but those publishers would not find the books economically viable if they paid higher advances and royalties, and they would argue that their whole operation depends on keeping their overheads down and on their ability to process the books as quickly as possible, and that means that they have neither the staff nor the time to give their authors the personal treatment that they really should have. In other words, the terms those publishers offer are fair in the light of the particular publishing job which they are doing. And they would point out that no author is obliged to accept the terms, and that there are many who do.

Finally, it is worth trying to understand why a publisher may not agree to all the changes in the contract which you ask for. Some publishers may be reluctant, for instance, to give you the right to be consulted about the jacket design. Why? Perhaps because they have suffered in the past from authors who think 'consultation' means 'a right of veto' or 'the right to conduct endless time- and money-wasting arguments, and to make impractical demands'. You should try to persuade them that you will not behave in that way, and that you will respect their professionalism and demonstrate your own.

Packagers

The contract between a packager and an author will differ in many respects from a normal publishing contract. One of the principal differences concerns the royalties, which will almost certainly be at lower rates. However, there is a major compensation: the packager sells the books to publishers at a royalty-inclusive price, and therefore you will receive your percentage whether or not the publisher sells a single copy; moreover you will be paid at the time the books are delivered to the publisher, or shortly thereafter; the same system will apply if the book is reprinted. If you should be commissioned to write a book by a packager, it will almost certainly be advisable to place the negotiations in the hands of an agent.

Poetry

If you publish a volume of poetry with one of the major publishing houses, everything included in this chapter so far will apply to the book. If, however, your work is published by one of the so-called 'Little Presses', you may not be called upon to sign a formal contract, but there should at least be some correspondence on the matter, and you should always ensure that this covers the copyright, which must remain in your possession. You may also receive only a token payment, or none at all, other than free copies of your work. The little presses often act as a showcase, and you may feel that it is worth accepting a minimal reward for that reason.

Articles

Word for word (and payment is usually by the word) the writing of articles can be far more lucrative than most literary work. You can earn a reasonable sum for a published letter, or for a single paragraph used as a 'filler'. Unless you are writing regularly for a journal, in which case you may have a formal contract, acceptance of an article for publication will usually be in the form of correspondence. The letter from the paper or magazine may, however, have many inadequacies – it may not name the fee, it may make no commitment as to when the article will be published, and it may not specify what rights the journal will have in the article. It is obviously preferable to sort these matters out right from the beginning. You should always ask for full NUJ rates – it is possible to obtain them even if you are a beginner – but be prepared for the fact that small, specialist magazines may laugh at the very idea, especially if you are an unknown writer. Payment is normally on publication, but some journals do not send out their cheques automatically, putting an obligation on the author to watch for publication of his or her work and to send in an invoice when the article appears; try to overcome this difficulty by getting the journal to agree that you will receive the fee on a given date, whether or not the article has been published by then. Do make sure that you do not grant a newspaper or magazine more than First Serial Rights (see page 111) – always retain your copyright.

Plays and Films

The theatre has an equivalent of the MTA in a Minimum Terms Contract which has been accepted by the Theatre Managers Association. Make sure that any contract you sign for the production of your play adheres to this MTC. It will almost certainly be worth your while to employ an agent. If your play is published, the publisher will pay you a royalty on copies sold, and will also act as a licensing and collecting agency, usually taking between 20% and 50% of the performance fees it receives.

Contracts for screenplays are so complex and come in so many varieties that you will certainly need expert advice, and should use one of the agents specializing in this business.

Radio and Television

The BBC and the independent television and radio companies work on standard rates and contracts. If you are working regularly in these media, it will pay you to join the Writers' Guild, which has particular interest and expertise in these fields, and in the cinema business, and which will be able to guide you in all the relevant contractual matters.

11   Proof-Reading

Although some magazines and newspapers do not send out proofs to their contributors, many do, and if your work is published in book form, it is virtually certain that you will be sent proofs and expected to return them promptly with any necessary corrections clearly marked.

Proofs come in several forms, the most common of which are galley proofs and page proofs. Galleys are long strips of paper on which the text appears in a single column, not having yet been divided up into pages; galleys are often used when it is expected that the text will be subject to heavy alterations, or for illustrated books which will not have the same amount of text on every page. Page proofs are the most usual form; as the name suggests, the text has been divided into the pages in which it will finally appear, and the proofs have often been bound with a paper cover, so that they really do look quite like a book.

Before many years pass, both typescripts and proofs will no longer be necessary. Authors will submit their books on word processor discs, all corrections will be made on the discs, and they will then go to the printer who will use them to produce the printed books. In the meantime, however, you will probably receive proofs for correction.

Proof-reading is a skilled job, and although you need not be too concerned if you are not practised at it, since someone at the publishing house will almost certainly be reading the proofs too and you are therefore not solely responsible, the more efficiently you can do the work the better.

Although you will probably be limited by the short time available for proof correcting, it is advisable to read your proofs at least twice yourself, and if possible to get other people to read them too. It is surprising how a different pair of eyes will see things that others have missed, and even the same pair of eyes, on a second reading, will find errors which they passed over the first time.

Your main task should be to look out for 'literals' – that is to say, errors in spelling, spacing, style of printing, etc. Don't think that these will be 'printer's errors' only – some may result from mistakes in your typescript which were never corrected, and others may have originated in the publisher's office. To find the literals you need to put your mind into a special mode in which, as you read the text, the brain looks at each individual word on its own, checking that it is correctly spelt. It is inevitably a fairly slow and laborious process, and it is important to prevent yourself, if you can, from becoming caught up in the sense of what you are reading to such an extent that you stop examining each word separately; it is all too easy to fall into the trap of reading what you think *ought* to be there, rather than what *is* there, especially if you have been checking the proofs already for a couple of hours and your eyes and brain are tired.

And that leads to the advice to do your proof-reading in short bursts, rather than in long sessions.

Always have a copy of the typescript with you while you are proof-reading. Check back, when you find a literal error, to see whether it is really the typesetter's mistake, or whether the error existed in the typescript. This is important because it will affect both the way you mark the change on the proof (see below) and the cost of the alteration.

I said earlier that your main task is to look for literals. What about the opportunity of making improvements to your text? There is usually quite a gap between acceptance of your work and its appearance in proof form, and when you first see it in print, it will have become slightly unfamiliar (at least, more so than when you were working on it every day), and it may produce in you very mixed feelings; you will undoubtedly feel pleased and proud, but I can almost guarantee that you will also experience a keen sense of disappointment. You will realize that you have not expressed this or that point with the clarity you had hoped for, that the style over which you laboured so long reads leadenly rather than with elegance, that you have repeated the same word six times on page 43, and that (oh, dear!) your heroine's green eyes have later turned blue.

So, yes, of course, while your brain is examining each word for literals, another part of it is aware of the sense of the material, and its style, and is trying to keep tabs on accuracy and consistency, and the overall effect. You are certain to find things that you want to change.

Don't alter them unless they are really essential, *because corrections are extremely expensive to make.*

You will probably have seen in your contract a clause which

states that you will be responsible for the cost of proof corrections over a certain percentage (very often 10%) of the cost of composition of the whole book. You might think that that was fine – that you would be able to change completely one page in every ten without involving yourself in any financial penalty – but it doesn't work like that. The charges for corrections to proofs are very high, and indeed the cost will often seem out of all proportion in relationship to the initial cost of composition. The typesetter is responsible for any errors that he has made, so you don't need to worry about those, but every other correction will be charged for, and it is therefore essential to get your typescript into as perfect a state as you can before it goes to the typesetter, and then to keep your corrections to the absolute minimum.

One tip which can save a lot of expense is to make sure that any alterations you make affect as few lines of type as possible. So if you delete a word, a phrase, a sentence, or indeed a whole paragraph, try to replace the material with something of exactly the same length. Equally, if you insert new wording, try to cut something which will make the exact amount of room for it. Naturally, it is not always possible to do this, and it is less essential if the change comes at the very end of a chapter, or sometimes in the last line of a paragraph, where there is space available for a certain amount of new material, but the object of the exercise is to avoid any need for the typesetter to shift large chunks of text around, especially if the moves are going to involve several pages.

Of course, there are some occasions when you simply have to make substantial alterations at proof stage. It is advisable to consult your publisher in such cases to explain why the changes are essential and how best to carry them out.

When you find anything in your proofs which needs to be altered, you should use the conventional signs, the more common of which are printed on the following pages. *The Writers' and Artists' Yearbook* contains a longer list of these signs, extracted from a document called *BS 5261: Part 2: 1976* which may be obtained from the British Standards Institution, 2 Park Street, London W1A 2BS. While it is advisable to use the accepted markings, the most important thing is that your corrections should be legible and your intentions unmistakable.

You will probably be sent two sets of proofs, one of which may be stamped to indicate that it is the 'marked set', together with your original typescript. The marked set will probably contain some corrections and possibly some queries (to ask, perhaps, whether something in the typescript is really intended to appear in that form). These marks, which have been made by the typesetter, should be in green ink. When you come to mark the proofs yourself, use a red pen for typesetter's errors, and blue or black for your own alterations.

Having incorporated all your corrections into the marked set, you will be required to return it to the publisher. You may retain the second set of proofs, and if you mark in them all the necessary changes, you will be able to check that they have all been carried out when the finished books eventually arrive.

Proof Reader's Marks

The symbols for correcting proofs are taken from a British Standard BS 5261: PART 2 1976 *Copy preparation and proof correction – Specification of typographic requirements, marks for copy preparation and proof correction, proofing procedure.* Extracts from the new Standard are reproduced below with the permission of BSI. Complete copies can be obtained from them at Linford Wood, Milton Keynes, Bucks., MK14 6LE. All authors, printers and publishers are recommended to adopt the new correction symbols.

	Textual Mark	Marginal Mark
Correction is concluded	None	/
Leave unchanged	_ _ _ _ _ _ under character to remain	Ⓙ
Push down risen spacing material	Encircle blemish	⊥
Insert in text the matter indicated in the margin	⋏	New matter followed by ⋏
Insert additional matter identified by a letter in a diamond	⋏	⋏ Followed by for example ⬦A
Delete	/ through character(s) or ⊢——⊣ through word(s) to be deleted	⌀

Instruction	Textual Mark	Marginal Mark
Delete and close up	through character or through character e.g. charaacter charaaacter	
Substitute character or substitute part of one or more word(s)	/ through character or through word(s)	New character or new word(s)
Wrong fount. Replace by character(s) of correct fount	Encircle character(s) to be changed	
Change damaged character(s)	Encircle character(s) to be changed	
Set in or change to italic	under character(s) to be set or changed	
Set in or change to capital letters	under character(s) to be set or changed	
Set in or change to small capital letters	under character(s) to be set or changed	
Set in or change to capital letters for initial letters and small capital letters for the rest of the words	under initial letters and under rest of word(s)	
Set in or change to bold type	under character(s) to be set or changed	
Change capital letters to lower case letters	Encircle character(s) to be changed	
Change italic to upright type	Encircle character(s) to be changed	

Instruction	Textual Mark	Marginal Mark
Invert type	Encircle character to be inverted	↻
Substitute or insert full stop or decimal point	/ through character or ∧ where required	⊙
Substitute or insert semi-colon	/ through character or ∧ where required	;
Substitute or insert comma	/ through character or ∧ where required	,
Start new paragraph		
Run on (no new paragraph)		
Centre	[enclosing matter to be centred]	[ ]
Indent		
Cancel indent		
Move matter specified distance to the right	enclosing matter to be moved to the right	

Instruction	Textual Mark	Marginal Mark
Take over character(s), word(s) or line to next line, column or page		
Take back character(s), word(s) or line to previous line, column or page		
Raise matter	over matter to be raised	
	under matter to be raised	
Lower matter	over matter to be lowered	
	under matter to be lowered	
Correct horizontal alignment	Single line above and below misaligned matter e.g. $mi_{sa}{}^{li}g_{n_e}d$	
Close up. Delete space between characters or words	linking characters	
Insert space between characters	between characters affected	
Insert space between words	between words affected	
Reduce space between characters	between characters affected	
Reduce space between words	between words affected	
Make space appear equal between characters or words	between characters or words affected	

12 The Published Author

The writing income of published authors is not necessarily restricted to the moneys paid to them by their publishers, and it is pleasing to find that other sources bring additional financial benefits.

Public Lending Right

Since 1979 you have been entitled by law to receive a Government-funded payment for borrowings of your books from public libraries in Britain. Once your book has been published, it is your responsibility to register it for PLR, and you can do so by applying to The Registrar, Public Lending Right Office, Bayheath House, Prince Regent Street, Stockton-on-Tees, Cleveland TS18 1DF. Any sums due to you are paid annually in February. You do not have to share PLR income with your publisher, and that applies equally to moneys which you may receive from ALCS (see below).

The principle of a Public Lending Right was first put forward in 1951 by John Brophy, who suggested a payment of 'A Penny a Book'. His efforts to secure this payment failed, but the campaign was revived in the 1970s by the Writers Action Group, with the additional support of the Society of Authors and the Writers' Guild. All authors should be grateful to Maureen Duffy and John Brophy's daughter Brigid, who were the leaders of the Writers Action Group, and whose tireless determination finally won the day.

When PLR became law in 1979, the Government allocated an annual sum of £2 million for its funding, and that sum has since been twice increased, so that it now stands at £3½ million. It may seem curmudgeonly to complain at this addition to the income of British authors, but the moneys available are quite inadequate. To begin with, the sum should now be over £4 million simply in order to have kept pace with inflation, and even that amount would allow for a payment of only very slightly more than 1p per borrowing, which does not begin to compare with the value of John Brophy's 1d in the 1950s. All authors have a duty to campaign for an increase in the funding by writing in the early autumn, when budgets for the ensuing year are under consideration, to the Minister for the Arts and to their own MP.

The Authors' Licensing and Collection Society

In Britain PLR is paid only to authors of British residence, but the PLR scheme in West Germany allows for payment to non-resident authors, provided that the sums due should be paid in bulk to an agency, which will then distribute the sums due to the various authors. Similarly, Belgian and Dutch television companies pay royalties on British television programmes which they broadcast under the system known as 'simultaneous cabling'. In Britain the collecting agency for these moneys is the Authors' Licensing and Collection Society (ALCS). If you are a member of either the Society of Authors or the Writers' Guild, you are automatically a member of ALCS. If you do not belong to either of those organizations, it may pay you to join as an individual member for the current annual fee of £5. You can do this by writing for details to Mrs Janet Hurrell, The General Secretary, ALCS, 7 Ridgmount Street, London WC1E 7AE. German libraries contain quite a large number of books in English, so even if your works are not translated into German, it could be worth joining ALCS. Moreover, PLR is a concept which is gradually being adopted in other countries, and ALCS will certainly be dealing in due course with the resulting payments for British authors.

The ALCS is also closely involved with the Copyright Licensing Agency. This agency exists to license photocopying of published work, which is illegal when unauthorized, except when the photocopied material is minimal in quantity and is for personal use only. It is against the law, unless you have specific written permission, to photocopy complete books or plays or other material, or even large parts thereof. The CLA was set up in 1982 and its main activities to date have been the licensing of various educational authorities, schools and colleges under a scheme whereby a record is kept of the material which has been photocopied, and a royalty paid per page. Half of the money goes to the publisher of the work in question, and the remainder is paid to ALCS, which in turn passes it on to the author concerned.

The CLA is working to extend the range of users of

photocopying machines covered by its scheme, and hopes, for instance, eventually to include the ubiquitous printshops.

The ALCS takes a small percentage from the sums it distributes as a handling charge, but the authors who constitute its council ensure that the whole operation is run with economical efficiency, so that the authors shall see as much of the money as possible.

Public Speaking

Authors of published books are sometimes asked to speak to various organizations. Many authors, despite wizardry with the written word, are inarticulate or inaudible, or both, but for others it may prove a useful addition to income. The Society of Authors and the Writers' Guild recommend that authors should charge a minimum fee of £50 for a public address, but this is unrealistic unless you are famous or unless you speak only to wealthy gatherings. If you speak to a Women's Institute or a Townswomen's Guild you cannot expect a payment of more than about £15, plus travelling expenses, and some organizations will offer less, or indeed nothing at all. Some authors also feel that they should not charge when speaking to a writers' circle, but if it is a professional engagement the labourer is surely worthy of his hire, however tiny the fee may be.

A speaking engagement does, of course, provide an author with useful publicity, and may stimulate sales of his or her books (or, more likely, additional borrowings from the public library), and this is undoubtedly in the minds of those who do not offer fees. In the same way, if you are given an interview on local radio in connection with the publication of a book you will probably not receive any fee, on the grounds that you have been given free publicity. Shame!

Selling Copies of Your Own Books

Most publishers' contracts include a clause allowing the author to buy copies of his work at trade terms, but forbidding their resale. However, you may wish to sell copies of your book at the full retail price at various functions you attend, and publishers will generally allow you to do so, provided that you seek their permission first. If you do sell books in this way, you may be depriving a bookseller of a sale, and you should take that into consideration, for authors need booksellers, many of whom make a precarious enough living. On the other hand, the total quantity of books that you sell privately is unlikely to be really significant.

Grants

The Regional Arts Associations will occasionally provide authors with financial assistance in the form of bursaries to underwrite research or simply to buy time for a proposed work (usually one which has already been contracted for by a publisher), especially if the project is of particular interest in the region concerned. The various RAAs are listed in *The Writers' and Artists' Yearbook*, and you should apply to your local Association for information on whether such grants are available, and how to apply.

Grants are also available in certain circumstances from a number of other sources, such as the Royal Literary Fund. Details can be found in *The Writer's Handbook*.

Prizes

In recent years literary prizes have proliferated, the most prestigious, such as the Booker and Whitbread Prizes, bringing their winners not only very substantial sums of money but vastly increased sales. In most cases, it is the responsibility of the publisher to enter books from his list for such awards, but some are open for entries direct from the author. A list of prizes is included in *The Writer's Handbook*.

Income Tax

All your earnings from your writings are subject to Income Tax, including any profit you make by selling at full price copies of your books which you have bought at trade terms. It is unwise, when you receive a nice cheque for your work, to go out and spend the lot – keep some in reserve for the dear old bloodsuckers of the Inland Revenue service.

The bloodsuckers are not, however, entirely unreasonable, and all your expenses in connection with your writing are chargeable against the income you receive from it. You should therefore retain all receipts for paper, typewriter ribbons, etc., and for any other expenses you incur, such as travel, purchase of reference books, postage, telephone, office furniture, secretarial services, and so on. It is also possible to claim for the use of a room in your house, if it is used only for your writing, and for a proportion of your lighting and heating bills. It is worth noting that if these expenses total more than the earnings you have received from writing, you will be allowed to offset the difference against your other income.

You can of course deal with your tax inspector directly – it will help you if you have kept meticulous records of everything that you have earned from your writing and everything that you have spent in achieving that income – but unless your earnings are minimal, it will probably pay you to employ a good accountant. Search around until you find one who has some knowledge of the way an author works and of those claims which a writer can make and which the Inland Revenue inspectors will consider to be legitimate. An author's income is irregular and unpredictable (except that you can always be sure that the money will come in rather later than you hoped), and a competent accountant will be able to arrange that your tax payments are, at least to some extent, evened out and paid over a period of time.

A good accountant is worth having, incidentally, especially if you a full-time professional writer, not only for tax purposes, but because he or she will be able to advise you on such matters as Social Security contributions, pension schemes for the self-employed, investments, etc.

Organizations for Authors

Writers regularly complain that theirs is a lonely occupation. We are, it sometimes seems to me, a somewhat discontented profession, always wittering on about the agony of writing, our insecurity, the inadequacy of our rewards, the lack of understanding even from our nearest and dearest, and, of course, the wickedness of publishers. It is largely nonsense, because most of us enjoy the work and would not want to do anything else. Perhaps we indulge in such self-pity simply as an expression of the artistic temperament. Nevertheless, we do like to meet fellow authors to discuss our common problems and to agree how hard done by we are, and because we discover that so many of them are charming and interesting people.

There are hundreds of societies and groups for anyone interested in writing, ranging from small local writers' circles to the Book Trust (formerly the National Book League) and such international organizations as PEN, and many authors find it very worthwhile to belong to several of them. A large number of them are listed in *The Writers' and Artists' Yearbook*.

There is no doubt, however, that the two outstanding associations, to which frequent reference has already been made in this chapter, are the Society of Authors and the Writers' Guild of Great Britain.

The Society of Authors was founded in 1884. It is the senior and larger of the two organizations, and its members represent every genre of writing. It contains specialist groups for translators, broadcasters, and educational, children's, technical and medical writers. For more than a hundred years it has worked with considerable success to improve the status of authors and to defend their rights.

The Writers' Guild was founded in 1959 as the Screenwriters' Guild, and although it too covers all forms of writing, it is still perhaps the prime association for those who work in television or films. It has separate committees dealing with writing for television and film, radio, theatre, and books.

The Society of Authors and the Writers' Guild are officially recognized as trade unions, but the Society is not affiliated to the TUC, whereas the Guild is.

Both organizations offer advice to their members on all matters connected with authorship, and there is a considerable degree of co-operation between them, so that they frequently negotiate jointly with government departments on such matters as VAT, PLR and copyright, and in discussing terms with the Publishers Association or with individual publishers, as, for example, in relation to the Minimum Terms Agreement. Representatives of the Society and the Guild serve on the council of ALCS. If the lot of authors has been greatly advanced in the last thirty years or so it is largely due to these combined efforts.

The Society and the Guild both produce regular publications for their members, arrange various social events, seminars and the like, and also offer a number of other benefits, ranging from facilities for buying stationery at favourable terms to pension schemes.

All authors should join one or other of these organizations. The qualifications for membership differ slightly, but publication or at least acceptance of material for publication is essential. The subscription to the Society of Authors is currently £50 per year, while the Guild charges a percentage of a member's income from writing, amounting at the time of writing to a minimum of £30 and a maximum of £480. Details can be obtained from The Society of Authors, 84 Drayton Gardens, London SW10 9SB, or from the Writers' Guild of Great Britain, 430 Edgware Road, London W2 1EH.

The Society and the Guild both have among their members writers whose prime interest lies in articles for magazines and newspapers. However, if you are such an author you may be interested in applying for membership of the Institute of Journalists, Bedford Chambers, Covent Garden, London WC2E 8HA, or the National Union of Journalists, Acorn House, 314 Gray's Inn Road, London WC1X 8DP.

Index